IN PARABLES

The Challenge of the Historical Jesus

In Parables

THE CHALLENGE OF THE HISTORICAL JESUS

John Dominic Crossan

1817

Harper & Row, Publishers, San Francisco
Cambridge, Hagerstown, New York, Philadelphia
London, Mexico City, São Paulo, Singapore, Sydney

The Scripture quotations are from the Revised Standard Bible and used by permission.

Extract from *Tiger at the Gates*, by Jean Giraudoux, trans. Christopher Fry, is cited by permission of Oxford University Press.

Extract from *Collected Poems* by Marianne Moore, copyright 1935 by Marianne Moore, renewed 1963 by Marianne Moore and T. S. Eliot, reprinted with permission of Macmillan Publishing Co., Inc.

Extract from *A Sky of Late Summer* by Henry Rago, copyright © Henry Rago 1962 (originally appeared in *Poetry*), reprinted with permission of Macmillan Publishing Co., Inc.

Extract from *Collected Poems* by William Butler Yeats, reprinted with permission of Macmillan Publishing Co., Inc., Mr. M. B. Yeats, the Macmillan Co. of London & Basingstroke and the Macmillan Co. of Canada Ltd.

(Continued on following page)

FIRST HARPER & ROW PAPERBACK EDITION PUBLISHED IN 1985.

Library of Congress Cataloging in Publication Data

Crossan, John Dominic
  In parables: the challenge of the historical Jesus.
  Includes bibliographies.
  1. Jesus Christ — Parables. I. Title
BT375.2.C76   226'.8'066   73–7067
ISBN 0-06-061606-7
ISBN 0-06-061609-1 (pbk)

83 84 85 86 10 9 8 7 6

For Margaret

Contents

Acknowledgments

1. Sources

The four chapters of this book originally appeared as articles in various scholarly journals. They have been completely rethought, revised, and rewritten for their present integrated presentation. Chapter 1, "Parables and the Temporality of the Kingdom," was published in an earlier and shorter version under the title "Parable as Religious and Poetic Experience," in *The Journal of Religion*, 53 (1973), pp. 330–358. Chapter 2, "Parables of Advent," was published as part of "The Seed Parables of Jesus," in the *Journal of Biblical Literature*, 92 (1973), pp. 244–266. Chapter 3, "Parables of Reversal," was published as "Parable and Example in the Teaching of Jesus," in *New Testament Studies*, 18 (1971–1972), pp. 285–307. Chapter 4, "Parables of Action," includes what originally appeared as "The Parable of the Wicked Husbandmen," in the *Journal of Biblical Literature*, 90 (1971), pp. 451–465. To this has been added a paper, "The Servant Parables of Jesus," which was presented to the Seminar on Parables of the Society of Biblical Literature in Chicago, 1973. The full text appeared in their Seminar Papers, 109th Annual Meeting, 1973. Grateful acknowledgment is made to the editors of these journals for permission to reprint in revised format what appeared in more technical style in their pages. Readers who are interested in working with the Greek text, with wider bibliographical data, and with the general apparatus of scholarship will be able to go to these source articles.

2. *Texts*

The biblical text used in this book is the *Revised Standard Version* but best read in *Gospel Parallels*, ed. B. H. Throckmorton, Jr. (3rd. ed.; Camden, N.J.: Nelson, 1969). Space does not allow the full citation of each parable and its variants, so such a text is presumed throughout the book. The non-biblical "Gospel of Thomas" will be cited from the edition of A. Guillaumont *et al.*, *The Gospel according to Thomas* (Leiden: Brill; New York: Harper & Row, 1959).

3. *Notes*

Two procedures replace footnotes. When an author is cited in the text and the reader may wish to locate the quotation, one can turn to the back of the book where the exact reference will be given under the appropriate pagination, but without any footnote number. Second, at a few important points in the argument, references will be made to numbered bibliographies. These will be found after the Notes at the back of the book. There will also be a short but very selective bibliography for the entire book.

4. *Quotations*

With the elimination of footnotes, frequent direct citations are placed in the text itself. This is a deliberate introduction of the partners in dialogue. Quotation is both an acknowledgment of intellectual debt and the presentation of a running bibliography.

Preface

Natives of poverty, children of malheur,
The gaiety of language is our seigneur.
(Wallace Stevens, "Esthétique du
Mal")

The subtitle of this book is "The Challenge of the Historical Jesus." The book is not concerned, however, with either the religion of Jesus or the faith of Jesus. Neither is it concerned with the psychological self-consciousness or even the theological self-understanding of Jesus. The term "historical Jesus" really means the language of Jesus and most especially the parables themselves. But the term is necessary to remind us that we have literally no language and no parables of Jesus except and insofar as such can be retrieved and reconstructed from within the language of their earliest interpreters. One might almost consider the term "Jesus" as a cipher for the reconstructed parabolic complex itself. This complex forms a systemic whole and can be studied as such even without knowing all the parables that were originally contained within it. We need to know only enough to understand their systemic unity. An expression such as, for example, "Jesus' experience of God," will mean within the context of this book no more and no less than the experience of God which is articulated within the parabolic system under study.

The title of this book is IN PARABLES. This deliberately reflects at least four levels of meaning. The most obvious one refers to the special linguisticality of Jesus' message which is summed up in Matt. 13:34: "All this Jesus said to the crowds *in parables;* indeed he said nothing to them without a parable."

A second understanding recalls the reinterpretation of Jesus' parabolic intention created by the primitive church and reflected, for example, in Mark 4:10–11: "And when he was alone, those who were with him with the twelve asked him concerning the parables. And he said to them, 'To you has been given the secret of the kingdom of God, but for those outside everything is *in parables,*' " or again in Mark 4:33: "He did not speak to them without a parable, but privately to his own disciples he explained everything." Here one imagines a certain in-group who alone understand the parables which are hidden from the comprehension of outsiders. To these latter they are inexplicable riddles. Like in-jokes, then, there are also *in-parables.* This restatement of intentionality is, of course, quite understandable. Jesus proclaimed God in parables but the primitive church proclaimed Jesus as the Parable of God. They did not experience God in the gaiety of language as Jesus had done and so his parables became for them what they could never have been for Jesus, rather expendable.

Third, and more important, the title summarizes the thesis that parables are only to be understood from inside their own world. They are revelatory of world only to insiders, not to any definite, predetermined in-group but to the group formed in them, to those who have learned to live *in parables.* In the words of Franz Kafka: "Why such reluctance? If you only followed the parables you yourselves would become parables and with that rid of all your daily cares. Another said: I bet that is also a parable. The first said: You have won. The second said: But unfortunately only in parable. The first said: No, in reality: in parable you have lost."

Finally, and most important, there is a fourth meaning already appearing behind this third one and it stands in the background of the book as well. This is the deliberate question of whether there is any other way to live and any other way to know reality than *in parables.* It evokes the possibility that "in reality" means no more and no less than "in parables," that reality is parabolic. The poets announce this explicitly. William Carlos Williams: "Only the imagination is real!/ I have declared it/ time without end." Wallace Stevens: "So, say that final belief/ Must be in a fiction." W. H. Auden: "Truth is knowing that we know we lie." So does Ronald Barthes, in bringing Leopold von Ranke's "just the facts" to its last and dying gasp: "The paradox comes full circle: narrative structure was evolved in the crucible of fiction (via myth and the first epics), yet it has become at once the sign and the proof of reality. It is clear that the attenuation (if not disappearance) of narrative in contemporary historians, who deal in structures rather than chronologies, implies much more than a change of school; it represents in fact a fundamental ideological transformation: historical narrative is dying: from now on the touchstone of history is not so much reality as intelligibility." And, to the extent that Werner Heisenberg speaks for science, so do the scientists: "The scientific method of analyzing, explaining and classifying has become conscious of its limitations, which arise out of the fact that by its intervention science alters and refashions the object of its investigation. In other words method and object can no longer be separated. The scientific world view has ceased to be a scientific view in the true sense of the word." When reality is seen as parabolic, as images projected on the white screen of chaos, the question of Jean Giraudoux in *Tiger at the Gates* comes forcibly to one's attention:

Helen: If you break the mirror, will what is reflected
         in it cease to exist?
Hector: That is the whole question.

There is, however, another and yet deeper question, and this is the question of Jesus. What is it that breaks our mirrors? What can we experience in the sound of their breaking glass and what can we glimpse in the cracks of their shattering?

A final word. One attempts a book on the parables of Jesus with a double diffidence. There is, first of all, the general awareness of the inevitable reduction involved in any commentary on any poetry. The ultimate function of such exegesis is to render itself unnecessary. As Martin Heidegger put it: "The final, but at the same time the most difficult step of every exposition consists in vanishing away together with its explanation in the face of the pure existence of the poem." But, secondly, there is a special problem with parables as such. One wonders what the maker of parables must think of the maker of comments. What would the parabolic mind say to the exegetical mind if, just for once, it had the chance? Maybe this, from Ezra Pound, to a cat too near his cage and a Possum too near his poetry: "Prowling night-puss leave my hard squares alone/ They are in no case cat food."

IN PARABLES

The Challenge of the Historical Jesus

What we have to deal with is a conception which is essentially simple but involves far-reaching consequences. It is that the parables of Jesus are not—at any rate primarily—literary productions, nor is it their object to lay down general maxims . . . but each of them was uttered in an actual situation of the life of Jesus, at a particular and often unforeseen point . . . they were preponderantly concerned with a situation of conflict. They correct, reprove, attack. For the greater part, though not exclusively, the parables are weapons of warfare. Every-one of them calls for immediate response.

The parable of the Prodigal Son is therefore not primarily a proclamation of the Good News to the poor, but a vindication of the Good News in reply to its critics . . . primarily an apologetic parable, in which Jesus vindicates his table companionship with sinners against his critics.

(J. Jeremias, *The Parables of Jesus*, pp. 21, 131, 132)

In writing poems, the author must use his *image* because he sees it or feels it, *not* because he thinks he can use it to back up some creed . . .

All poetic language is the language of exploration. Since the beginning of bad writing, writers have used images as ornaments. The point of Imagism is that it does not use images as ornaments. The image is itself the speech. The image is the word beyond formulated language.

The image is not an idea. It is a radiant node or cluster; it is what I can, and must perforce, call a VORTEX, from which, and through which, and into which, ideas are constantly rushing.

(Ezra Pound, *Gaudier-Brzeska, A Memoir*, pp. 99, 102, 106)

INTRODUCTION: THIRTEEN
WAYS OF LOOKING
AT A PARABLE

You almost hear fingerprints
Graft and take root
Like tiny galaxies;
The Other Intelligence
Trying the doorknob.
    (Thomas Johnson, *Poetry*, 120 (1972), p. 136)

What we need to know is how the imagination thinks. Or, to turn it another way, how the human being thinks with his imagination; how he thinks in pictures.
    (Elizabeth Sewell, *The New Orpheus*, p. 367)

You cannot tell people what to do, you can only tell them parables; and that is what art really is, particular stories of particular people and experiences . . .
    (W. H. Auden in M. K. Spears, *The Poetry of W. H. Auden*, p. 13)

The important philosophic task is to rescue metaphor from the manipulators of the psychological image and restore it to its relevant ontological status.
    (R. Jordan, *Sewanee Review*, 67 (1959), p. 22)

nor till the poets among us can be
    "literalists of
    the imagination"—above
      insolence and triviality and can present

for inspection, "imaginary gardens with real toads in them,"
    shall we have
  it.
(Marianne Moore, *Collected Poems*, p. 41)

Whoever can give his people better stories than the ones they live in is like the
priest in whose hands common bread and wine become capable of feeding the
very soul, and he may think of forging in some invisible smithy the uncreated
conscience of his race.
    (Hugh Kenner, *The Pound Era*, p. 39)

A poet's function—do not be startled by this remark—is not to experience the
poetic state: that is a private affair. His function is to create it in others. The
man of genius is the one who infuses genius into me.
    (Paul Valéry in W. C. Booth, *The Rhetoric of Fiction*, p. 376)

I cordially dislike allegory in all its manifestations, and always have done so since
I grew old and wary enough to detect its presence. I much prefer history, true
or feigned, with its varied applicability to the thought and experience of readers.
I think that many confuse "applicability" with "allegory"; but the one resides
in the freedom of the reader, and the other in the purposed domination of the
author.
    (J. R. R. Tolkien, *The Lord of the Rings*, I, p. xi)

The author makes his readers . . . if he makes them well—that is, makes them
see what they have never seen before, moves them into a new order of perception
and experience altogether—he finds his rewards in the peers he has created.
    (Wayne C. Booth, *The Rhetoric of Fiction*, pp. 397–398)

"Born to say one thing,"
All the books for the one word:
The metaphor not means but end,
Not the technique
But the vocation, the destiny.
    (Henry Rago, *A Sky of Late Summer*, p. 54)

And the wonder and mystery of art, as indeed of religion in the last resort, is
the revelation of something "wholly other" by which the inexpressible loneliness
of thinking is broken and enriched.
    (Wallace Stevens, *Opus Posthumous*, p. 237)

Accordingly, the existing languages in which we find ourselves "thrown" are always open to orientation towards this aboriginal language which "speaks" in silence. And it is to our creative poets and thinkers that we look to find the words which somehow intimate the ineffable, old and familiar words long in use made to speak anew their relationship with the very source of language.

(T. Kisiel, *Heidegger and the Path of Thinking*, p. 95)

Do not forget that a poem, even though it is composed in the language of information, is not used in the language-game of giving information.

(L. Wittgenstein in K. T. Fann, *Wittgenstein's Conception of Philosophy*, p. 26)

one

PARABLES
AND THE TEMPORALITY
OF THE KINGDOM

> The mules that angels ride come slowly down
> The blazing passes, from beyond the sun.
> Descensions of their tinkling bells arrive.
> These muleteers are dainty of their way.
> Meantime, centurions guffaw and beat
> Their shrilling tankards on the table-boards.
> This parable, in sense, amounts to this:
> The honey of heaven may or may not come,
> But that of earth both comes and goes at once.
> Suppose these couriers brought amid their train
> A damsel heightened by eternal bloom.
> (Wallace Stevens, "Le Monocle de Mon
> Oncle")

The new quest for the historical Jesus has by now almost twenty years of research behind it. Its methodological principles are quite clear and coherent, at least in theory, and they seem the most adequate ones for the type of materials presented in the gospel accounts. The methodology can be summarized in five steps (see Bibliography 1). First, the careful and comparative reading of the same data in the gospels of Mark, Matthew, and Luke makes quite obvious the amount of creative reinterpretation which these latter two authors allowed themselves even when they had a written source before them. Recent study of Mark himself has also indicated how creatively he revised and rephrased his own sources. This constant creativity on the Jesus tradition presents us with layer upon layer of interpretative restatement before and even after written accounts started to appear. When one raises questions concerning the historical Jesus one cannot ignore the immediate problem posed by this situation. It is from this problem and for this situation that the methodology has been devised.

Second, then, one must first bracket any immediate discussion on historicity and authenticity because one does not even have a definite saying on which to pass such judgments. One has a multiform saying or story and if one wishes some absolute principle such as, "unhistorical until proved historical," or, conversely, "historical until proved unhistorical," one ignores the fact that there is often no single form of the saying to which such principles can be applied. What, or which, of the versions of a given story or saying is historical or unhistorical until proved the opposite? Hence, the second step is the deliberate bracketing of any decision for or against authenticity and historicity on the level of the historical Jesus.

Third, one must attempt to write a history of the transmission of the piece of tradition under discussion. This will trace its successive steps of development and will isolate its earliest form.

Fourth, it is this earliest form that can now be appraised in terms of historical authenticity for Jesus. Since creative reinterpretation by the primitive church is the presupposition of the whole problem, a rigorous negativity must be invoked to separate what Jesus said or did from what the tradition records of his words and deeds. One must look especially for divergence between this earliest form and the general attitude of the primitive church. Only when such can be discerned can one be methodologically sure that it stems from the historical Jesus and not from the creativity of the church. This will be all the more secure when the original saying has been reinterpreted back toward Judaism in the usage of the earliest Jewish Christianity itself. In such cases one can see the radicality of Jesus being muted back into normalcy.

Fifth, this "criterion of dissimilarity" just invoked will apply not only to subject and content but even more especially to style and to form. One is especially interested in forms of expression which are peculiar to Jesus and with which the primitive church does not seem to be too much at home.

One example may clarify all this theoretical exposition. Take the saying of Jesus concerning the Pharisaic request for a sign as found in the three Synoptic Gospels:

The Pharisees came and began to argue with him, seeking from him a sign from heaven, to test him. And he sighed deeply in his spirit, and said, "Why does this generation seek a sign? Truly, I say to you, no sign shall be given to this generation."

(Mark 8:11–12)

When the crowds were increasing, he began to say, "This generation is an evil generation; it seeks a sign, but no sign shall be given to it except the sign of Jonah. For as Jonah became a sign to the men of Nineveh, so will the Son of man be to this generation. . . . The men of Nineveh will arise at the judgment with this generation and condemn it; for they repented at the preaching of Jonah, and behold, something greater than Jonah is here."

(Luke 11:29–32)

Then some of the scribes and Pharisees said to him, "Teacher, we wish to see a sign from you." But he answered them, "An evil and adulterous generation seeks for a sign; but no sign shall be given to it except the sign of the prophet Jonah. For as Jonah was three days and three nights in the belly of the whale, so will the Son of man be three days and three nights in the heart of the earth. The men of Nineveh will arise at the judgment with this generation and condemn it; for they repented at the preaching of Jonah, and behold, something greater than Jonah is here."

(Matt. 12:38–41)

Here one cannot begin with questions of authenticity because we have three versions to work with. Which one is to be judged authentic or inauthentic as a saying of Jesus? In summary form, the history of the transmission is as follows. Stage 1 is Mark 8:11–12 which is an absolute and unconditional denial of the request. The denial does not appear so sharply in the English translation but in Greek the form of the Hebraic oath is still quite visible. The Greek reads literally: "*if* a sign shall be given to this generation." This is a standard way of avoiding the full form of a sworn statement: "(May God strike me down) *if* a sign shall be given to this generation." Those who take God and language seriously are chary about what might happen in the pause between the two halves of the oath. Maybe God might take the first half at the speaker's word before the second one was ever uttered! Such a refusal under oath hardly allows exception and one is not surprised that the oath form is totally absent from Luke and Matthew: "if" is replaced by "not" in the Greek. Stage 2 is seen in Luke 11:30–32 and Matt. 12:41–42 which qualifies Jesus' absolute denial by offering the sign of Jonah. At this stage the sign of Jonah has to do with preaching and repentance: as Jesus to this generation so Jonah to the Ninevites. Stage 3 appears only in Matt. 12:40 and specifies the sign of Jonah in a way completely different from that in Stage 2: as Jonah was in the whale for three days so will Jesus be in the tomb three days. So, one comes finally to ask the question with which historical Jesus research is concerned: is Stage 1 from Jesus or from the church and placed by it on the lips of Jesus? In this case the answer is a strong affirmation of authenticity. This absolute and sworn denial of a sign is quite different from the attitude of early Christianity (see Stages 2 and 3, for example) and, in effect, these later stages seek to move Jesus' radical denial back toward Judaism and its interest in signs.

The validity of this methodology will be presumed throughout this book. But the "criterion of dissimilarity" will be applied here to the form as well as to the content of Jesus' words. The interest will be on Jesus' use of metaphor in sustained parabolic form and on how this is distinct from the usage of the primitive church and also contemporary Judaism. Certain hermeneutical problems of a very basic and far-reaching nature have surfaced in recent work on the parables which demand that the exegete move into what may be unfamiliar territory in the fields of philosophy and poetry. In seeking to understand and explain the historical Jesus certain conceptual categories hitherto taken for granted seem more and more inadequate to articulate properly the meaning of Jesus' message. It is with this problem that the book will be concerned.

I. The Form of Jesus' Parables

The Hebrew term *mashal* and its Septuagint translation *parabolē* refer to a very broad field of language and the use of this latter term in the New Testament is just as general. It includes almost any type of figurative language from the short riddle to the long and fully developed allegory. This is obviously too general a classification to be of much exegetical assistance and one needs to establish more precisely the types and classes within this wider usage. In more technical terms, what exactly is the *form* of figurative speech which Jesus is using or, in other words, if we call it "parable" how is this to be understood?

It must be remembered that *form* as used in form-critical methodology is not just a unit of tradition as formed in a certain linguistic structure, but this as formed in and by and for a definite situational function. If this is true for the forms created in and by the primitive communities, it is also true for forms used by the historical Jesus himself. If we can ascertain his use of a certain form, the discussion must be a matter not only of style but of situation, not only of form but of function.

1. *Allegory and Parable*

For the moment an allegory will be considered as a story in figurative language whose several points refer individually and collectively to some other event which is both concealed and revealed in the narration. An example is the story of the great eagle told by the prophet Ezekiel which refers to the king of Babylon. Every major element of the allegory in Ezek. 17:3–10 is later interpreted step by step in 17:11–21. This seems to be exactly what Jesus does in the story of the Sower in Mark 4:3–8 as interpreted point by point in 4:14–20. With such a warrant, apparently stemming from Jesus himself, and with so many other allegorical interpretations present in the synoptic tradition, it is quite understandable that the term "parable" be taken to mean allegory. Hence the traditional interpretation of this form as used by Jesus was that it represented allegory and needed careful point by point decoding. But by the end of the last century Adolf Jülicher had challenged this view and claimed that Jesus' stories were not allegories with many separate but connected references but were parables with one main point incarnating some very general religious and ethical truth. The first half of this assertion became the basis for very successful research in the following years and this served to prove that the second half was inaccurate. If each parable contained only one central point this was to be interpreted not in terms of general religious truth but in the very specific terms of Jesus' own historical situation and eschatological message.

At this point the major distinction between allegory and parable seems to have become rather mechanical and rationalistic. An allegory has many separate but connected points of reference and each detail is important in itself, but the parable has only one major point and all the details serve only to build up this single reference. It was almost inevitable that a distinction so formulated would eventually be questioned. The possibility that allegory, with its many points, and parable, with its single point, were but ends of a sliding scale within which one had to talk of parabolic allegories or allegorical parables began to be discussed by the second half of this century.

It is at this very point that the suspicion of totally inadequate conceptualization begins to be felt and one wants to reopen the entire discussion on a more profound level than the counting of one, more, or many points of reference. This suspicion is heightened when one recalls the insistence with which some of our greatest poets have stressed the tremendous difference between allegory and symbol and when one contrasts this with the presumed combination of allegory and symbol in Jesus' parables.

Four examples will have to suffice, but the stature of the poets involved will serve to underline the problem. Goethe expressed the distinction of allegory and symbol in terms of expressing the inexpressible: "Allegory transforms the phenomenon into an abstract concept, the concept into an image, but in such a way that the concept can still be expressed and beheld in the image in a clearly circumscribed and complete form. Symbolism transforms the phenomenon into an idea, the idea into an image, in such a way that the idea remains for ever infinitely active and unreachable in the image and, even if expressed in all languages, still inexpressible." This is very similar to the norm of difference found in Yeats: "Symbolism said things which could not be said so perfectly in any other way, and needed but a right instinct for its understanding; while Allegory said things which could be said as well, or better, in another way, and needed a right knowledge for its understanding. The one gave dumb things voices, and bodiless things bodies; while the other read a meaning—which had never lacked its voice or its body—into something heard or seen, and loved less for the meaning than for its own sake." On the other hand, the poet Coleridge emphasizes the symbol's participation in its referent as the heart of the distinction: "An allegory is but a translation of abstract notions into a picture-language, which is itself nothing but an abstraction from objects of the senses. . . . On the other hand a symbol . . . is characterized by the translucence of the special in the individual, or of the general in the special, or of the universal in the general. Above all by the translucence of the eternal through and in the temporal. It always partakes of the reality which it renders intelligible; and while it enunciates the whole, abides itself as a living part in that unity, of which it is the representative." Much the same sort of difference is noted by Eliot in contrasting Charles Williams and Chesterton: "Chesterton's *The Man Who Was Thursday* is an allegory; it has a meaning which is meant to be discovered at the end; while we enjoy it in reading, simply because of the swiftly moving plot and the periodic surprises, it is intended to convey a definite moral and religious point expressible in intellectual terms. It gives you ideas, rather than feelings, of another world. Williams has no such 'palpable design' upon his reader. His aim is to make you partake of a kind of experience that he has had, rather than to make you accept some dogmatic belief."

These four citations serve to sharpen the problem. If there is a great chasm fixed between allegory and symbol, on which side of the divide are we to locate the parables of Jesus? One disclaimer may be in order before proceeding. In this book there is no presumption that the term "allegory" has a pejorative connotation or that allegory is a bad or inferior literary form, for Jesus or for anyone else. The only question is whether Jesus' stories *are* allegories in whole or in part, and if not, what are they?

2. Parable and Metaphor

Some recent works on the parables of Jesus have insisted on the necessity of treating them as literature and placing special emphasis on their relationship to the world of poetic metaphor (see Bibliography 2). This would seem to be a definite step in the right direction but, of course, it will not help to locate Jesus' parables in the world of poetic metaphor unless one knows more or less accurately what this latter means. The next step will be to investigate poetic metaphor to see whether a clearer idea of its identity helps the understanding and interpretation of Jesus' parables.

(1) Metaphor and Confusion. If one starts from a dictum such as Ludwig Wittgenstein's, "What can be said at all can be said clearly; and whereof one cannot speak thereof one must be silent," it might easily be concluded that metaphor's main purpose or, at least, inevitable result is confusion and obfuscation. In this view the poet is seen as an inadequate prose writer or scientist, and the extended poetic creation of myth and mythology is viewed as pseudoscience or protoscience to be swept away by the reality it so dimly and dangerously foreshadowed. Even when and where it is not spelled out as crudely, or as honestly, as this, the idea is that metaphor and its world are, at very best, part of the infancy of mankind.

Against such conclusions which would dismiss metaphor as useless if not harmful stand assertions by both poets and philosophers that it is irreplaceable and irreducible. The poet Henry Rago asserted the inviolability and uniqueness of metaphor in various essays. "To be a poet at all is to be present to the ontology that is hidden in words. And what shall we say of metaphor? We might begin with the definitions we were taught as children, seeing it as a mere figure of speech rather than as speech itself, as a depth of speech that is otherwise impossible." And again: "There is the metaphor that is less a metaphor, because it is the metaphor I choose; there is the metaphor that is more deeply, irrevocably a metaphor, because it chooses me . . . What is the metaphor as we see it now? No mere figure of speech, but the transmutation that itself is poetry: a matter of content: the style that is the man."

In a section which echoes the words of Goethe, Coleridge, Yeats, and Eliot cited above, the philosopher Paul Ricoeur insists that "An allegory can always be *translated* into a text that can be understood by itself; once this better text has been made out, the allegory falls away like a useless garment; what the allegory showed, while concealing it, can be said in a direct discourse that replaces the allegory. By its triple function of concrete universality, temporal orientation, and finally ontological exploration, the myth has a way of *revealing* things that is not reducible from a language in cipher to a clear language." But why is poetic metaphor so irreplaceable, irreducible, and indispensable?

(2) Metaphor and Ornament. One of the critical heritages of the last two centuries would claim that metaphor is important because of its function for elegance and ornamentation. It decorates and adorns what

could be said in unadorned but equally sufficient prose language. Hugh Kenner has suggested that this heritage is still very much with us: "The approach to language of Descartes, Locke, and Kant, which makes the poet at best an embroiderer of familiar sentiments with suitable emotive accessories ('What oft was thought but ne'er so well expressed') has still a powerful grip on our interpretative procedures." Cleanth Brooks has noted that even a poet himself might accept this critical theory while denying it in his own poetic practice. He can quote one poet, Robert Frost, saying that "Poetry is metaphor." But he can also find another one, A. E. Housman, asserting that "Metaphor [is] inessential to poetry." But even if one intuitively opts for the former alternative, one has not yet described very clearly what poetic metaphor actually is.

(3) Metaphor and Illustration. Any good teacher knows the value of metaphor in explaining to a student something which is new to one's experience. The metaphor illustrates the information which the teacher wishes to impart to the student. C. S. Lewis described this situation very accurately: "On the one hand, there is the metaphor which we invent to teach by; on the other, the metaphor from which we learn. They might be called the Master's metaphor, and the Pupil's metaphor. The first is freely chosen; it is among many possible modes of expression; it does not at all hinder, and only slightly helps, the thought of its maker. The second is not chosen at all; it is the unique expression of a meaning that we cannot have on any other terms; it dominates completely the thought of the recipient; his truth cannot rise above the truth of the original metaphor." In this case the Master does not really need the metaphor and is simply using it as a pedagogical device. The Pupil only needs it until he can attain to the level of the Master's comprehension when he too will disregard it. In such a case the information which the Master has is quite clear to the Master before, apart from, and without its metaphorical expression. The referent of the discourse depends on the metaphor only accidentally because of the exigencies of the teaching situation on the part of the Pupil. When metaphor illustrates information one graduates from metaphor. In any final analysis such metaphors are intrinsically expendable. Metaphors are pedagogic cocoons.

(4) Metaphor and Participation. None of the preceding intends to deny that metaphor can be used for confusion. One is aware of that special type of nonthinking in which everything is, in a certain sense,

everything else. It is against such obfuscation that Ezra Pound's aphoristic line must stand in warning: "Oak leaf never plane leaf." Nor does it deny that metaphors are often used for sheer ornamentation. Wallace Stevens repeatedly skewered such usages, metaphorically, as "fops of fancy," or "bawds of euphony," or "pimps of pomp." Neither is it to deny the use of metaphor for pedagogic illustration. But it is still to ask if that is all there is to it?

The thesis is that metaphor can also articulate a referent so new or so alien to consciousness that this referent can only be grasped within the metaphor itself. The metaphor here contains a new possibility of world and of language so that any information one might obtain from it can only be received *after* one has participated through the metaphor in its new and alien referential world. In such a case the speaker is not the Master using metaphor only for some Pupil's sake. Rather the referent is Master, the speaker too is Pupil, and the necessary classroom is the metaphor. Remove the metaphor and you lose the referent. The metaphor is body, not cocoon.

When a metaphor contains a radically new vision of world it gives absolutely no information until after the hearer has entered into it and experienced it from inside itself. In such cases the hearer's first reaction may be to refuse to enter into the metaphor and one will seek to translate it immediately into the comfortable normalcy of one's ordinary linguistic world. Herbert Marcuse has expressed very clearly this problem for poetry: "The poet might answer that indeed he wants his poetry to be understandable and understood (that is why he writes it), but if what he says could be said in terms of ordinary language he would probably have done so in the first place. He might say: Understanding of my poetry presupposes the collapse and invalidation of precisely that universe of discourse and behavior into which you want to translate it." From the outside it may sound quietly or even stridently insane. One must risk entrance before one can experience its validity.

It is especially with metaphors which seek to express what is permanently and not just temporarily inexpressible, what one's humanity experiences as Wholly Other, that this primacy of participation over and before information is most profoundly relevant. The Wholly Other must always be radically new and one can experience it only within its metaphors. Here it is not a question even of imagining at the limits of one's imagination but rather of imagining wholly new ways of imagining. In the distinction of Michel Foucault, it is a question not of "utopia" but of "heterotopia," and indeed of dwelling in permanent heterotopia: *"Utopias* afford consolation. . . . *Heterotopias* are disturbing, probably because they secretly undermine language. . . . That is why utopias permit fable and discourse: they run with the very grain of language and are part of the fundamental dimension of the *fabula;* heterotopias (such as those to be found so often in Borges) desiccate speech, stop words in their tracks, contest the very possibility of grammar at its source; they dissolve our myths and sterilize the lyricism of our sentences."

One might object that even such metaphors can become fossilized as their new vision becomes accepted and commonplace, and one begins to think that it is not *a* way but *the* way, the one and only and true way of seeing things, things as they are and without the blue guitar. But even in such cases one is usually dealing with dormancy rather than with death. As Ezra Pound, inventing Chinese poetry for our time, read in Fenollosa: "But the great thing to remember is that all this poetry was once in the language itself, and still underlies the dry bones of even our dictionaries. Every word, a metaphor, perhaps several degrees deep, still has the power to flash meaning back and forth between apparently divergent and intractable planes of being." We are much more aware of this revival process in the creativity of the artistic symbol than we are in the case of poetic metaphor but it is just as true for both. A visit to the Paleolithic cave-paintings of the Dordogne valley should be sufficient to discover that old and dead are alien terms in the world of art. T. S. Eliot saw them and said: "Art never improves, but the material of art is never quite the same." If art can survive advertising and poetry politics, we may again be able to appreciate that what once was radically new in symbol or metaphor is always latently powerful to create and inspire another and different radical newness.

In summary, then, on the last two uses of metaphor, the ones which really concern us in this book: there are metaphors in which information precedes participation so that the function of metaphor is to illustrate information about the metaphor's referent; but there are also metaphors in which participation precedes information so that the function of metaphor is to create participation in the metaphor's referent. It is in this sense that one might interpret the distinction between allegory and symbol cited earlier from Goethe, Coleridge, Yeats, and Eliot. This would also be the difference in the two meanings of metaphor quoted from Henry Rago, and in the distinction of allegory and myth noted by Paul Ricoeur. It is surely this latter type of metaphor which Wallace Stevens intended with "A poet's words are of things that do not exist without the words."

3. *Metaphor and Structure*

At this point it may be helpful to solidify the terminology which will be presumed from now on in this book. There is nothing apodictic or even axiomatic about this usage. It is the distinctions involved and not their titles that are at stake. Figurative language, if one will permit what seems a necessary redundancy at this point in time, talks about one subject and intends another $(A=B)$. When fossilized it can be called literal language $(A=A, B=B)$ which is probably a contradiction in terms, as Owen Barfield has been saying for years. Figurative language has two quite different functions. One is to illustrate information so that information precedes participation. The other is to create participation so that participation precedes information. The former function produces allegories and examples, pedagogic devices which are intrinsically expendable. The latter produces *metaphor* on the verbal level and *symbol* on the nonverbal level. At their best they are absolutely inexpendable and even at their worst they are dormant rather than dead. This book is only interested in the verbal phenomenon of metaphor, and not in symbol. Here a further distinction may be helpful. Metaphor can appear as either parable or myth. For our present purpose the difference may be underlined by borrowing a famous line from Marianne Moore and using it rather out of context. A *parable* gives us "imaginary gardens with real toads in them." A myth gives us imaginary gardens with imaginary toads in them. A parable tells a story which, on its surface level, is absolutely possible or even factual within the normalcy of life. A myth tells one which is neither of these on its surface level. In parable one talks of the very real road between Jerusalem and Jericho; in myth one talks of centaurs in a dragon world. The distinction is useful but not of course absolute. There is always Tolkien where one can see real shadows in the land of Mordor. But, for now, parable is a metaphor of normalcy which intends to create participation in its referent. It talks of A so that one can participate in B, or, more accurately, it talks of x so that one can participate in X and so understand the validity of x itself. Its structural pattern is X-in-x, and the hyphens are not dispensable.

No attempt is being made to use a term such as "participation" as if it were a magic wand to solve all the problems of metaphor. The term is invoked to stake out an area of thought and to suggest a direction for study. Such a fuller study would involve an ontology, or even an anti-ontology in the Heideggerian sense, which grounds adequately such a theory of participation. It would also require great attention to the structuring of metaphor, to how it can create this world rather than that one, to how it can create new world and not just repaint the same old tired one we know (Rebecca West: "A copy of the universe is not what is required of art; one of the damned thing is ample"). The metaphor which creates world is linguistic art at its most profound and indispensable moment. T. S. Eliot summed up its function in this manner: "For it is ultimately the function of art, in imposing a credible order upon ordinary reality, and thereby eliciting some perception of order *in* reality, to bring us to a condition of serenity, stillness, and reconciliation; and then leave us, as Virgil left Dante, to proceed toward a region where the guide can avail us no farther." The quotation can stand even though one might well wonder if "credible order" is not "reality" itself, and if one really ever travels without a Virgil or if such hopes are but instances of what Allen Tate called the "angelic" fallacy.

It should be clear, however, that this function of linguistic art, of metaphor, cannot be effected without structure. It is structure alone whereby metaphor can offer us *this* new world rather than *that* one to participate in. So the "credible order" of which Eliot spoke is actually an "imposing of structure," as Sheldon Nodelman has noted: "Every work of art has the dual role not only of 'expressing'—that is, more accurately, of synthesizing—a total world-view or global state of consciousness, but also of actively transforming the consciousness of the observer, of imposing its structure upon him, and of forming, as part of a collectivity of other works, a 'language' of artistic form, which conditions, in terms of its presuppositions and possibilities, the perception of every individual. This language, continually in the process of modification and reshaping by individuals, nevertheless is always the necessary ground upon which such reshaping may occur."

4. *Structure and Experience*

There is still one more point to be noted before we can return to the specific metaphorical language of Jesus. Within the understanding of metaphor just argued, it is now necessary to discuss the relationship between the poetic experience and its metaphorical expression, and also to compare this experience and expression with that of religion.

(1) Poetic Experience. At the heart of poetry is the poetic experience itself and it is the poet's vocation so to articulate this event metaphorically that the referent of the experience is contained and incarnated in it. Poets themselves know the struggle of doing this adequately, and that when it is greatly successful it has been deeply paid for. Even when one makes allowance for romantic *Sturm und Drang* on the autobiographical level, the message has still a compelling validity. William Butler Yeats discussed one of his creations in terms of sleepless nights and almost speechless days, and whatever one may think of this, one is still persuaded by his sober conclusion: "It is not inspiration that exhausts one but Art." The appearance of spontaneity and simplicity does not necessarily mean that experience and expression were simultaneous, but only that the former has driven laboriously and successfully to full expression. As Yeats himself put it elsewhere:

> I said: "A line will take us hours maybe;
> Yet if it does not seem a moment's thought,
> Our stitching and unstitching has been nought."

Because it is the experience, and indeed the experience's referent, which must control and direct the expression, the destiny of both artist and poet is circular, or in Eliot's words:

> We shall not cease from exploration
> And the end of all our exploring
> Will be to arrive where we started
> And know the place for the first time.

This is true not only for the hearer but also for the poet. Only in one's metaphor does one experience its referent. For, as was seen earlier for poetic metaphor, the referent is Master and we are all Pupils in this case.

To quote one final time from Yeats: "It is so many years before one can believe enough in what one feels even to know what the feeling is."

We are children of this century and we want to ask the possibly impossible questions: how can one know authentic poetic expression? what are the crieria whereby one recognizes with certitude the presence of the great artist or the great poet? The philosopher Maurice Merleau-Ponty answered this in one example: "By his painting [Renoir] himself defined the conditions under which he intended to be approved." A great poet or a great artist is one who establishes in and by and through his work new criteria for artistic or poetic greatness by establishing a new world in which it *is* such. One can always have criteria afterward, when they are not really needed; one never has them beforehand, when they would be really useful. So on the deepest level the initial questions are meaningless. A true metaphor is one whose power creates the participation whereby its truth is experienced. This is clearly the hermeneutical circle at its most circular, the epistemological spiral wound down to its tightest tension. A sensitive critic can always comment on the adequacy of the expression, and a sensitive philosopher can guard the gift of the experience, but the final word must still be: He who has eyes to see, let him see. One recalls the warning of Northrop Frye that: "The presence of incommunicable experience in the center of criticism will always keep criticism an art, as long as the critic recognizes that criticism comes out of it but cannot be built on it." On the day we have prior criteria for genius, be it artistic, poetic, philosophical, or religious, we shall no longer need either forever.

(2) Religious Experience. There is no intention in this book of confusing poetry and religion. It is clear, for example, that the world for which and to which Jesus is speaking is the world of religious experience. Yet it is becoming increasingly clear that the specific language of religion, that which is closest to its heart, is the language of poetic metaphor in all its varied extension. There is apparently some peculiar appropriateness or even necessity for poetic expression and religious experience to walk so often hand in hand. This is true of the Bible in general and, as we shall see, of the parables of Jesus in particular. If the core of religion is the experience of the Wholly Other, one could no doubt talk about it and probably lose it in the process. But one might also be conscious that the experience demands and even creates its own form of expression

in which it becomes incarnate and present both nonverbally in symbol and verbally in metaphor. In that case the analogy between poetic and religious experience is obvious and their combination in the same person becomes a very precious gift. In both cases the experience-as-gift and the expression-in-metaphor are combined at the heart of the event, and in both cases the former's terminal gift is the successful completion of the latter. In a recent work on the language of religion, but using symbol for what we have been calling metaphor, Thomas Fawcett emphasized this combination. "The moment of perception, therefore, cannot really be separated from its symbolic formulation because the subject can never speak of his experience without the use of symbol . . . The ability to symbolize the experience derives from the experience itself, for in a sense it provides its own form of expression."

5. *Experience and Expression*

It is now time to return to the parables of Jesus. All the preceding could be accepted by someone who might still insist that Jesus' stories, to use a neutral term, are pedagogic figures (allegories, examples) rather than poetic metaphors (parables) as defined above. Indeed one might clinch the argument with two statements. First, the early church certainly accepted them often as examples and allegories. Second, such didactic and allegorical stories are completely within the tradition of Palestinian rabbinical teaching methods. The former point is not contested here, but the question of their original function as spoken by Jesus himself still stands. However, it is with the second objection that the next step is concerned.

(1) Expression in Jesus' Parables. The argument is that the rabbinical figures are didactic and pedagogical and are part of a teaching situation very often associated with a very specific text of Scripture or with a very particular problem in ethical living. They are examples to illustrate a dogmatic proposition. Two cases will suffice.

During the Feast of Sukkoth, also called Booths or Tabernacles, the last of the three great pilgrim feasts of Israel, celebrated in September–October at the end of the fruit harvest, one was supposed to "dwell" in artificial huts of branches instead of one's regular abode. But what if it rained heavily? "Throughout the seven days (of the Feast) a man must make his *Sukkah* a regular abode and his house a chance abode. If rain fell, when may he empty out (the *Sukkah*)? When the porridge would spoil. They propounded a parable: To what can it be compared?—to a slave who came to fill the cup for his master and he poured the pitcher over his face." The point of the story is quite obvious and its use is also quite expendable: if it rains it is a punishment from God! This answer can be put quite clearly in nonmetaphorical language, at least within the dogmatic presuppositions of the religion in question. The story serves only as illustration for information quite clear without and before it.

A second case concerns a problematic text of Scripture. The Ten Commandments do not appear until Exodus 20 and the all-important words, "I am the Lord thy God," appear in Exodus 20:2. But why are they not the very first lines of the Bible? "Why are the Ten Commandments not said at the beginning of the Torah? They give a parable. To what may this be compared? To the following: A king who entered a province said to the people: 'May I be your king?' But the people said to him: 'Have you done anything good for us that you should rule over us?' What did he do then? He built the city wall for them, he brought in the water supply for them, and he fought their battles. Then when he said to them: 'May I be your king?' They said to him: 'Yes, yes.' Likewise, God. He brought the Israelites out of Egypt. . . ." The story continues in parallel so that at its end it is quite clear why God "waited" until Exodus 20:2 to become and be accepted as Israel's king. Once again the story illustrates prior dogmatic information which could be expressed in nonmetaphorical language.

In both these cases it is clear that we are dealing with didactic stories poised somewhere between example and allegory but inevitably linked to the problem of life or text in a very precise and specific fashion. In any final analysis such figures are quite expendable and are only of value for pedagogical purposes.

But the evidence would indicate that Jesus' stories stem from a very different usage. They are not linked to specific biblical texts which need interpretation nor to precise moral situations for which they represent allegorical exemplification. This is not an attempt to exalt Jesus above the rabbis as an exercise in Christian chauvinism. It is to insist that they are doing completely different things. Their stories are didactic figures, those of Jesus are poetic metaphors; theirs are subservient to the teaching situations, those of Jesus are subservient only to the experienced revelation which seeks to articulate its presence in, by, and through them. It is neither necessary nor advisable to turn difference into hierarchical order. The teacher and the poet go different ways, but if one wishes to insist that Jesus was a teacher one must add that he taught as a poet!

This distinction has been pointed out already by Günther Bornkamm: "The rabbis also relate parables in abundance, to clarify a point in their teaching and explain the sense of a written passage, but always as an aid to the teaching and an instrument in the exegesis of an authoritatively prescribed text. But that is just what they are not in the mouth of Jesus, although they often come very close to those of the Jewish teachers in their content, and though Jesus makes free use of traditional and familiar topics. Here the parables are the preaching itself and are not merely serving the purpose of a lesson which is quite independent of them." One might summarize the entire purpose of the present book by stating that it seeks to render explicit all that is contained in that final phrase, "the parables are the preaching itself," especially in the light of the parallel assertion of Ezra Pound, cited in this book's epigraph, that, "the image is itself the speech."

(2) Experience in Jesus' Parables. It has been argued that *figures* (figurative language) can move toward either illustrating information on their referent (examples, allegories) or creating participation in their referent (metaphors, symbols), and that metaphors are to examples and allegories, on the verbal level, as symbols are to signs, on the nonverbal level. In the terminology of this book *metaphor* is, in effect, verbal symbol and will be used in this restrictive sense hereafter. So also with *parable.* It will be used restrictively to denote metaphor structured within normal "reality," as distinct from myth, where normal "reality" can be ignored. It has also been argued that the rabbinical figures are examples and/or allegories but that Jesus' figures are not of this type. They are rather poetic metaphors, and are parables of normalcy, not myths of metanormalcy. In other words, and at the risk of confusing terms all over again, we are placing Jesus' parables within that world of expression which Paul Ricoeur terms "symbol," using it in a wider sense than does this book: "Unlike a comparison which we *look at* from the outside, the symbol in fact is the very movement of the primary meaning

which makes us share the hidden meaning and thus assimilates us to the thing symbolized, without our being able to get hold of the similarity intellectually."

The present point concerns the creative relationship between experience and expression when one is dealing with metaphor, and especially with parables rather than myths. In effect the question is this: what does such a mode of expression tell us of the experience that begot it? This is not an attempt to probe the self-consciousness of Jesus or to infect the whole discussion with an invalid psychologism. Erik Erikson's comment in discussing Luther can serve as a warning and a verdict on a century of research into the historical Jesus: "It is necessary, however, to contemplate (if only as a warning to ourselves) the degree to which in the biography of a great man 'objective study' and 'historical accuracy' can be used to support almost any total image necessitated by the biographer's personality and professed calling."

Poetic experience terminates only with its metaphorical expression so that the two are inseparably linked. So also religious experience involves both "the moment of disclosure or perception itself" and "the embodiment of the experience in symbolic form," to quote from Thomas Fawcett. This means that the experience and the expression have a profound intrinsic unity in the depths of the event itself. The fact that Jesus' experience is articulated in metaphorical parables, and not in some other linguistic types, means that these expressions are part of that experience itself. This is a most delicate area, for the religious and poetic imagination and creativity have their own mysterious alchemy of generation and transformation. Possibly one assertion can suffice for the moment. There is an instrinsic and inalienable bond between Jesus' experience and Jesus' parables. A sensitivity to the metaphorical language of religious and poetic experience and an empathy with the profound and mysterious linkage of such experience and such expression may help us to understand what is most important about Jesus: his experience of God. That Jesus spoke in metaphorical parables, as defined above, is important both for an understanding of his experience and of that experience's referent itself for which such linguisticality was appropriate. One is immediately aware that experience so expressed is quite likely of another world from that which is articulated, for example, in the figures of the book of Revelation, the Apocalypse of John.

II. The Function of Jesus' Parables

One of the few conclusions of research into the historical Jesus on which most scholars agree concerns the Kingdom.

1. *Parables and Kingdom*

There is very wide agreement that Jesus is the one who proclaimed the Kingdom of God. This summary statement of Norman Perrin is illustrative of the consensus: "The central aspect of the teaching of Jesus was that concerning the Kingdom of God. Of this there can be no doubt and today no scholar does, in fact, doubt it. Jesus appeared as one who proclaimed the Kingdom; all else in his message and ministry serves a function in relation to that proclamation and derives its meaning from it."

(1) Kingdom as Divine Action. A term such as "Kingdom" tends, however, to place a very different emphasis for us than would the original Aramaic term of which it is a somewhat unhappy translation. The word designates for us primarily a place or region; it includes subjects and, at least potentially, a king. But the primary emphasis of the original Semitic term was not the *place*, but the *act* of God in which kingly rule and dominion was clearly manifested. The parallels in Psalm 145:11–12 make this evident:

> They shall speak of the glory of thy kingdom,
>   and tell of thy power,
> to make known to the sons of men thy mighty deeds,
>   and the glorious splendor of thy kingdom.

The poetic parallelism in these verses indicates that Kingdom is to be understood as power and as mighty deeds. We can quote once again from Norman Perrin: "The Kingdom of God is the power of God expressed in deeds; it is that which God does wherein it becomes evident that he is king. It is not a place or community ruled by God; it is not even the abstract idea of reign or kingship of God. It is quite concretely the activity of God as king."

(2) Kingdom and Eschatology. Another point on which there is general scholarly agreement is that the Kingdom of God is an eschatological expression, that is, that it pertains to a teaching concerned with world-ending. It is at this point that the problems begin to multiply. The understanding of Jesus' term "Kingdom of God" as indicating ending-of-world has gone through three major interpretations in the last hundred years.

The first (thesis) is represented by Albert Schweitzer and is usually termed *consequent eschatology:* Jesus taught that the Kingdom would arrive soon in the imminent end of the world. For example, Schweitzer interpreted the seed parables as meaning that, "the time of the sowing is past at the moment when Jesus speaks . . . the Kingdom of God must follow as certainly as harvest follows seed-sowing."

The second (antithesis) major position is that of C. H. Dodd who opposed this view and maintained that the Kingdom had already arrived in the words and deeds of Jesus. The position is usually called *realized eschatology* and the following sentences are indicative of its thrust: "Jesus declares that this ultimate, the Kingdom of God, has come into history," and again: "Whether its subsequent span would be long or short, men would henceforth be living in a new age, in which the Kingdom of God, His grace and His judgment, stood revealed."

Finally (synthesis), it seemed that these two disparate views had been reconciled in a third position, associated especially with Joachim Jeremias. This argued that Jesus taught "an eschatology that is in process of realization," what we might term, *progressive eschatology*. One might exemplify this by saying that the death and resurrection of Jesus was like D-Day and the parousia of Christ would be V-E Day. At this point it seemed a secured conclusion that there was a present-future tension in Jesus' understanding and use of the phrase "Kingdom of God." This tension is indicated accurately in the terse summary of James M. Robinson: "the message of Jesus consists basically in a pronouncement to the present in view of the imminent eschatological future."

(3) Eschatology and Linear Time. This established consensus has been very badly undermined in recent research. The present-future tension was sapped at one basic level by the claim that sayings concerning the future return of the Son of Man on the lips of Jesus did not come from the teaching of the historical Jesus but were placed there by the

primitive church. In other words, the clearest and most direct interest in the imminent (or even distant) future did not come from Jesus at all (see Bibliography 3). Other sayings with a clear future orientation have not fared much better. For example, Norman Perrin has argued very persuasively that Mark 9:1, " 'Truly, I say to you, there are some standing here who will not taste death before they see the kingdom of God come with power,' " is a redactional creation by Mark himself and does not stem from the historical Jesus even though placed on his lips. This constant and increasing loss of the future polarity in the supposed present-future tension of Jesus' teaching has led to the suggestion that Jesus may not have been talking at all in our concept of linear time and that any present and/or future polarity is quite inadequate to his intention.

The suggestion that Jesus was not speaking within linear time is not in itself new. What would be very new is an attempt to take it with utmost seriousness. It has tended to be mentioned at the end of articles and books where it remains a hermeneutical intuition rather than being placed up front where it would have to become an exegetical principle. Ten years ago Norman Perrin noted: "We may not interpret the eschatological teaching of Jesus in terms of a linear concept of time, for this is foreign to the prophetic understanding to which he returns." More recently, Robert Funk brought up the problem of Jesus' understanding of temporality and warned against the "confusion of objectivity and lack of conceptual sophistication." In other words, the interpretation of eschatology, history, and time present in Jesus' teaching of the Kingdom is again a very open question, and it is *our* presumption that linear time is the only temporality possible which is being placed under question.

(4) Prophetic and Apocalyptic Eschatology. It is not enough to say that Jesus' understanding of Kingdom was eschatological. There are two major ways in which the tradition whence Jesus came might have interpreted eschatology. There was an older prophetic eschatology and a more contemporary apocalyptic eschatology. For our present purpose this distinction rests on two contrasts. First, prophetic eschatology was concerned with an ending of world, while apocalyptic looked to *the* ending of *this* world. Second, the former had no concept of another world above or beyond this one (for example, heaven), while the latter

could only accept the ending of this one so easily because it envisaged a far better one elsewhere. In other words, ending a world and destroying the globe were not necessarily correlative in all of Israel's traditions. Or, as Bruce Vawter put it recently: "Whatever is to be said of the contention that a yearning for immortality is innate in man, responding to the very nature of his being, it seems to be both a fact and a fortunate fact that most of Israel's history was played out in a society which had eschewed this yearning." In ordinary, everyday speech we are well aware of the use of world, as distinct from globe, in such phrases as, "one's world came to an end," or, more widely, "it was the end of an era, an epoch, a world." The question that all this raises, and raises most forcibly, is *whether Jesus is speaking out of the ancient prophetic eschatology precisely in order to oppose and deny the current apocalyptic eschatology of his contemporaries?*

Only two examples will be given here in positive answer to this programmatic question. The analysis of the parables is the major reason for its affirmation. Jesus' announcement of the Kingdom in prophetic eschatology as against the contemporary Jewish *and* early Christian consensus on apocalyptic eschatology is shown very clearly in Luke 17:20–24: "Being asked by the Pharisees when the kingdom of God was coming, he answered them, 'The kingdom of God is not coming with signs to be observed; nor will they say, "Lo, here it is!" or "There!" for behold, the kingdom of God is in the midst of you.' And he said to the disciples, 'The days are coming when you will desire to see one of the days of the Son of man, and you will not see it. And they will say to you, "Lo, there!" or "Lo, here!" Do not go, do not follow them. For as the lightning flashes and lights up the sky from one side to the other, so will the Son of man be in his day.' " Two divergent views of world and time and God clash in this simple juxtaposition. In 17:21 sign-seeking is invalidated by the historical Jesus because the Kingdom is already present, but in 17:22–24 sign-seeking is forbidden because the Son of Man will arrive in the future too swiftly for any such calculations. The thesis is that Jesus is proclaiming what might be termed *permanent eschatology*, the permanent presence of God as the one who challenges world and shatters its complacency repeatedly.

A second example arises from a contrast of Luke 11:20, "But if it is by the finger of God that I cast out demons, then the kingdom of God has come upon you," with the story of the Rich Man in Mark 10:17–22. In the former case the possessed man is liberated and the Kingdom is present as God shatters his demonic world. In the latter case the *Rich Man* can only experience the Kingdom if his world is shattered into poverty. Be it the world of demonic possession, of enriched security, or, elsewhere, of Pharisaic righteousness, the Kingdom is that which in shaking man's world at its foundations establishes the dominion of God over and against all such worlds.

Jesus was not proclaiming that God was about to end *this* world, but, seeing this as one view of world, he was announcing God as the One who shatters world, this one and any other before or after it. If Jesus forbade calculations of the signs of the end, it was not calculations, nor signs, but end he was attacking. God, in Kingdom, is the One who poses permanent and unceasing challenge to man's ultimate concern and thereby keeps world free from idolatry and open in its uncertainty. It should be quite clear that this raises some terribly basic questions which can only be indicated but not even faced at this point. Was apocalyptic eschatology breakdown or breakthrough for Israel's ancient prophetic eschatology? Is Jesus' prophetic eschatology reconcilable with the contemporary Jewish and early Christian emphasis on apocalyptic eschatology? And, in a few very simple words, is immortality a fundamentally idolatrous conception?

2. *Parables and Time*

It has been argued that Jesus' understanding of the Kingdom reverted to prophetic eschatology in order to deny the validity of contemporary apocalyptic eschatology. (One of my students, who will be rewarded with anonymity, has rephrased this distinction, not at all inaccurately, as pathetic versus apoplectic eschatology.) It was also seen that the difference between these two views was ultimately a divergent understanding of primordial temporality. It is now necessary to suggest how such an "other" view of time is to be imagined.

(1) Time and Prophecy. We can begin with the following quotation from Gerhard von Rad. It will be cited at some length because of the precision with which it formulates the problem. "The question of the specific way in which Hebrew thought understood time and history

brings us to an area of great importance for the correct understanding of the prophets. Earlier exposition was quite unaware that there was a problem here, and uncritically assumed that its own Western and Christian concept of time also held good for Israel. To-day, however, we are beginning to realise that her experience of which we call time and ours are different. Yet this in itself does not bring us very much further forward, for we find it extremely difficult to move beyond the terms of our own concept, which we naively believe to be the only possible one, and to understand the specific details of another in such a way as to be able to make much in reconstructing it. The attitude of Western man to linear time is, generally speaking, naive; time is seen as an infinitely long straight line on which the individual can mark such past and future events as he can ascertain. This time-span has a mid-point, which is our present day. From it the past stretches back and the future forwards. But to-day one of the few things of which we can be quite sure is that this concept of absolute time, independent of events, and, like the blanks on a questionnaire, only needing to be filled up with data which will give it content, was unknown to Israel." One could hardly ask for a clearer statement of the problem.

The heart of the difficulty is not just to imagine a different view of time but to do so when one has been conditioned to think that the past-present-future is the *only* way in which time can be imagined. We are like viewers trying to imagine the color excellence of, say, RCA as it is being advertised and demonstrated on our own Zenith color television. There are moments, however, when even our everyday and "naive" version of temporality shows certain strains. We can see time objectively outside ourselves and measurable by clocks and calendars and stars. It is a river in which we can specify our own position; it is a railroad, Eliot's "metalled ways of time past and time future," on which we have but to locate our station while other stops are behind us and new ones already apparent ahead. But there are moments when one wonders about this *present* which is encroached upon by the past up to the very point when it is arching into the future and so disappears before our very eyes save as the timeless intersection of past and future. Or one thinks about this *past* when one reads revisionist history, when the Old Frontier has already lost much of its luster and even the New Frontier is already beginning to tarnish, and one wonders what sort of objectivity this past really has. Or again, there are projections of the *future* and one is horrified to consider not how wrong they probably are but the possibility of using force and violence to insure their accuracy even if necessary by genetic manipulation. Finally, there are those moments when one hears or even repeats quite glibly that we are *all* conditioned by time and history, and then wonders, if *all,* then who is left to condition time and history and where do they come from? It is at such times that we hear what Yeats called "the cracked tune that Chronos sings" and consider investigating the cracks.

(2) Time and Poetry. Since our problem is how to imagine a different way of imagining time we must begin with the poets where, at least, the problem is not exactly news. Dilys Laing's poem "The Apparition" talks of the present:

> All is prepared in darkness. Enormous light
> is but the foetus of big-bellied night.
> The image hatches in the darkened room:
> the cave, the camera, the skull, the womb.
> Future and past are shut. The present leaps:
> a bright calf dropped between two infinite sleeps.

One is inclined to agree for, after all, the word "present" has such a good sound, conjuring up not only the now but the now as gift. However, one knows also the tyranny of nowism, of dominant fad, of relevance demanded to what may be but passing fancy (Wallace Stevens: "One cannot spend one's time in being modern when there are so many more important things to be"). One can also imagine a present which is no present, a now which is no gift. Stephen Spender's "Time in Our Time" invokes a very different image:

> Oh save me in this day
> when Now
> Is a towering pillar
> of dust which sucks
> The ruin of a world
> into its column.

The problem will not simply disappear by a sacramental invoking of the present. In summarizing Hans-Georg Gadamer's philosophical hermeneutics, Richard Palmer says: "There is no pure seeing and understanding of history without reference to the present. On the contrary, history is seen and understood only and always through a consciousness standing in the present." Again one agrees but only to return to the insistent question of David Jones in "The Anathemata":

> I do not know!
> I do not know!!
> I do not know what time is at
> or whether before or after
>   was it when—
> but when *is* when?

There is the question at its clearest: "when *is* when?"

In turning from statements of the problem to attempts at an answer, we can begin with one line of W. H. Auden from "For the Time Being." It is striking in its aphoristic clarity: "Time is our choice of How to love and Why." What is given here in a single line is one of the major themes of T. S. Eliot's "Four Quartets" as the poet "Measures time not our time . . . a time/Older than the time of chronometers." His vision has been summarized by Malcolm Ross: "In these poems the concepts of beginning and end become concepts of value, purpose, destiny rather than merely chronological concepts. And the intuition of eternity is made to possess and to illuminate the personal and the historical levels of the time process." But possibly it was Ezra Pound who, in Canto 92, put the answer most forcibly:

> Le Paradis n'est pas artificiel
>   but is jagged
> For a flash,
>   for an hour
> Then agony,
>   then an hour,
>   then agony
> Hilary stumbles, but the Divine Mind is abundant
>   unceasing
>   *improvisatore*
> Omniformis
>   unstill.

Paradise is not artificial, is not what Wallace Stevens termed "that Salzburg of the skies." We read that God is at work in history with a definite plan moving toward its profound consummation: salvation history on the model of Detroit's assembly line with God as Supreme Mechanic. Yet God's presence in history might well be like that of Art, something ever active but without plan or consummation, without clear development or steady improvement. We might be dealing with what should be visualized as neither static circle nor ascending line but rather as spokes coming out from a wheel's core. God does not act *in* history or intervene *in* time. It is the presence of God which, in calling to us for response, creates our history and gives us time, this history and this time. Time is, in both senses, the present of God.

(3) Time and Philosophy. It may be helpful to see how the poetic imagination of true human time has been conceptualized in philosophy. The understanding of time in this book is based on the constant probing of ontological time in the thought of Martin Heidegger, from *Being and Time* in 1927 to "Time and Being" in 1962. Theodore Kisiel has drawn attention to the specific images in which Heidegger discusses the advent of Being which creates the time of authentic humanity: "The language of *coming and going,* used to express the dynamics between man and Being. On the basis of such descriptions, *Ereignis* becomes the event of the advent of Being overcoming man through intervention in his ventures. Certainly no ordinary event, limited to a moment or period of time, but one that is momentous and periodic, or better, that which makes events momentous and periodizes them." This summary statement is of special importance because it underlines Heidegger's use of "coming" for the advent of Being in *Ereignis,* a sequence which is very helpful as a philosophical aid in understanding Jesus use of "coming" for the advent of God in Kingdom.

At this point one may feel and object that everything is starting to disappear into some atemporal and nonhistorical empyrean. History and time are not being ignored but grounded. One's authentic and primordial time does not come from the ticking of clocks and the wheeling of stars. These might only record anguished meaninglessness as one moves steadily toward suicide. Human time and human history arise from response to Being which comes always out of the unexpected and the unforeseen, which destroys one's planned projections of a *future* by asserting in its place the *advent* of Being. Its advent discloses a very different *past* from that which was taken for granted as objectively given before this advent. It may well involve the radical reappraisal and even *reversal* of that past. But it is this advent and this reversal which constitutes the force and power of a *present* which is now really and truly an *action*. Instead of the objective and surface succession of three moments in past-present-future, one now receives a deeper and more ontological simultaneity of three modes in advent-reversal-action.

With this view of human temporality it is clear how Heidegger could insist on the historicity of Hölderlin's poetry and yet not mean this in the sense that the poet merely echoes the relevant fads of his chronological moment. He says in his essay on "Hölderlin and the Essence of Poetry": "Hölderlin writes poetry about the essence of poetry—but not in the sense of a timelessly valid concept. This essence of poetry belongs to a determined time. But not in such a way that it merely conforms to this time, as to one which is already in existence. It is that Hölderlin, in the act of establishing the essence of poetry, first determines a new time." And we know from a poem of Heidegger's own that this time is the time in which

> We are too late for the gods and too
> early for Being. Being's poem
> just begun, is man.

(4) Time and Parables. It is against this understanding of temporality and historicity that the parables of Jesus will be interpreted in this book. They express and they contain the temporality of Jesus' experience of God; they proclaim and they establish the historicity of Jesus' response to the Kingdom. This does not mean that they are timeless truths or metahistorical models. But, on the other hand, they do not so much fit into a given historical situation as create and establish the historical situation of Jesus himself. There is, of course, more to Jesus' life than the parables which express its ontological ground. He was not crucified for parables but for ways of acting which resulted from the experience of God presented in the parables. In this regard the parables are cause and not effect of Jesus' other words and deeds. They are not what Joachim Jeremias called "weapons of warfare"; they are the cause of the war and the manifesto of its inception. In summary: as against Jülicher, the parables are not timeless moral truths beyond all and above all historical situations; but, as against Jeremias, neither are they to be located *in* Jesus' own historical experience as visual aids to defend a

proclamation delivered before them and without them. Jesus' parables are radically constitutive of his own distinctive historicity and all else is located in them. Parable is the house of God.

We are now ready to step more directly into the parabolic world of Jesus. Where should one begin? The French structuralist psychiatrist, Jacques Lacan, has noted that "one has only to listen to poetry . . . to hear a true polyphony emerge, to know in fact that all discourse aligns itself along the several staves of a score." The full parabolic proclamation of Jesus will be envisioned here on this musical analogy so that any one parable is only fully heard within the total melody of all those we can still hear. But while this must be maintained throughout the study, it does not tell one how or where to begin.

At this point another structuralist analogy may be of even more assistance. In his study of myths involving categories such as raw/ cooked, fresh/decayed, moistened/burned, etc., Claude Lévi-Strauss used a myth of the Bororo Indians of Central Brazil as what he termed his "key myth," or paradigmatic, reference myth. This was "chosen not so much arbitrarily as through an intuitive feeling that it was both rich and rewarding, and then, after analyzing it . . . I establish the group of transformations for each sequence, either within the myth itself, or by elucidation of the isomorphic links between sequences derived from several myths originating in the same community. This itself takes us beyond the study of individual myths to the consideration of certain guiding patterns along a single axis." We shall accept this procedure as a model and begin with what can be described as the "key parables" of Jesus. These are three parables which show most clearly the deep struc- ture of the Kingdom's temporality and which contain in themselves the entire parabolic melody: they are key, overture, paradigm; they are above all what Maurice Merleau-Ponty called "la parole originaire."

One preliminary note. In discussing Jesus' parables we shall be using not only the canonical gospels of Mark, Matthew, and Luke, but also the noncanonical "Gospel of Thomas," hereafter abbreviated as Gos. Thom. This is a Coptic Gnostic collection of Jesus' sayings discovered near Nag Hammadi in central Egypt around 1945. This text contains some parables not present in the canonical gospels and some very inter- esting variations on others present in both sources. It may well be likely that some parables appear in a more original version in this text than in the canonical versions and, in any case, this must always be reckoned with as a possibility in seeking to establish the original versions of parables (see Bibliography 4).

The three key parables to be studied as paradigmatic references are: the Treasure, in Matt. 13:44; the Pearl, in Matt. 13:45; and the Great Fish, in Gos. Thom. 81:28—82:3.

The first two parables are seen together in a rather harmonized version in Matt. 13:44–45: "The kingdom of heaven is like treasure hidden in a field, which a man found and covered up; then in his joy he goes and sells all that he has and buys the field. Again, the kingdom of heaven is like a merchant in search of fine pearls, who, on finding one pearl of great value, went and sold all that he had and bought it." The structural sequence of the two stories can be underlined by noting the main verbs: finds-sells-buys. We are confronted, for example in the Treasure parable, with a man whose normalcy of past-present-future is rudely but happily shattered. The future he had presumably planned and projected for himself is totally invalidated by the *advent* of the Treasure which opens up new world and unforeseen possibilities. In the force of this advent he willingly *reverses* his entire past, quite rightly and wisely he sells "all that he has." And from this advent and this reversal he obtains the Treasure which now dictates his time and his history in the most literal and concrete sense of these words. It gives him a new world of life and *action* he did not have before and he could not have programmed for himself. One feels that the Paul who wrote of his conversion in Gal. 1:16–18 would absolutely understand such a temporality and would even find its structure mirrored geographically in his own sequence of place: Damascus–Arabia–Jerusalem.

The same historicity of the Kingdom appears in Gos. Thom. 81:28 —82:3 but now with definite gnostic overtones: "And He said: 'The Man is like a wise fisherman who cast his net into the sea, he drew it up from the sea full of small fish; among them he found a large (and) good fish, that wise fisherman, he threw all the small fish down into the sea, he chose the large fish without regret.' " Here the temporality of advent-reversal-action can be seen reflected in the main verbs: found-threw-chose. But once again the pattern is clear although the image does not reflect the magnitude of the life-change involved in the Treasure and Pearl situations. Having obtained this one large fish, or, more likely, in order to obtain it more securely, the fisherman "threw all" the others back and grasped the happy gift of the large one.

These are surely humble and everyday examples and yet they are startling in their implications. It has always been clear that Jesus criticized many of the options open to the religious experience of his contemporaries: the Sadducees, the Pharisees, the Zealots, the Essenes. But usually, and especially since Paul and the Reformation, it is his critique of Law that is to the forefront. It is here suggested that the basic attack of Jesus is on an idolatry of time and that this is the center whence issued forth what Yeats called that "Galilean turbulence" which set Jesus against all the major religious options of his contemporaries. It should also be quite clear that he forged a two-edged sword which strikes as lethally against his contemporary Judaism as it should have done against primitive Christianity; thereafter it was much too late. The one who plans, projects, and programs a future, even and especially if one covers the denial of finitude by calling it God's future disclosed or disclosable to oneself, is in idolatry against the sovereign freedom of God's advent to create one's time and establish one's historicity. This is the central challenge of Jesus. The geographers tell us we do not live on firm earth but on giant moving plates whose grinding passage and tortured depths give us earthquake and volcano. Jesus tells us that we do not live in firm time but on giant shifting epochs whose transitions and changes are the eschatological advent of God. It is the view of time as man's future that Jesus opposed in the name of time as God's present, not as eternity beyond us but as advent within us. Jesus simply took the third commandment seriously: keep time holy!

In their totality, then, the parables proclaim the Kingdom's temporality and the three simultaneous modes of its presence appear most clearly in the key parables just noted. In a book of this length it is impossible to study all of Jesus' parables and yet when one discusses only a few the reader inevitably wonders if the dice have been loaded before the game began. Would it really work if all the parables were seen in detail? This question determines the procedure. Michel Foucault subtitled his study of the seventeenth and eighteenth centuries "An Archaeology of the Human Sciences." We can borrow his term and call the rest of this book an archaeology of the parables of Jesus.

The next three chapters will be devoted to parables which emphasize each of the three modes of the Kingdom's temporality: its *advent* as gift of God (II), its *reversal* of the recipient's world (III), and its empowering to life and *action* (IV). In each chapter we shall first suggest all those parables which could be studied under that heading and then investigate a few for each category in greater detail.

two

PARABLES
OF ADVENT

There might be in the curling-out of spring
A purple-leaping element that forth

Would froth the whole heaven with its seeming-so,
The intentions of a mind as yet unknown,

The spirit of one dwelling in a seed,
Itself that seed's ripe, unpredictable fruit.
    (Wallace Stevens, "Description Without Place")

It may be helpful to begin with a quotation from Ezra Pound which serves both as warning and challenge for this whole chapter: "I believe that the proper and perfect symbol is the natural object, that if a man uses 'symbols' he must so use them that their symbolic function does not obtrude; so that *a* sense, and the poetic quality of the passage, is not lost to those who do not understand the symbol as such, to whom, for instance, a hawk is a hawk." We have also heard from critics of "the decline of the figural imagination," in Nathan Scott's apt phrase, and so it will be necessary to tread very carefully in this section. We are not exactly attuned to the semiotics of the natural symbol.

1. *Advent and Joy*

In the triple but simultaneous modality of the Kingdom in the key parable of the Treasure, ontological primacy belonged to the *advent*, to the finding of the treasure itself. It was from this that all else flowed and it was this that determined new time and new history for the discoverer. The first group of parables to be considered are those which develop this theme. One can distinguish, but hardly separate, three different strands within this advent: hiddenness and mystery ("hidden" in Matt. 13:44a), gift and surprise ("found" in 13:44b), discovery and joy ("joy" in 13:44c). The parables of advent will stress one or another of these three strands.

Hiddenness and mystery are in the forefront in the parables of the budding Fig Tree (Mark 13:28; Matt. 24:32; Luke 21:29–30) and the Leaven (Matt. 13:33; Luke 13:20–21; Gos. Thom. 97:3–6). One cannot see summer but, especially in contrast with its nondeciduous neighbors in Palestine, the budding of the fig tree is the epiphany of its advent and its presence. So also one cannot see the leaven ("hidden" in Matt. 13:33 and Luke 13:21) but the swelling of the bread makes it evident to all that it was there.

Gift and surprise are underlined in the parables of the Sower (Mark 4:3–8; Matt. 13:3–8; Luke 8:5–8; Gos. Thom. 82:3–13) and the Mustard Seed (Mark 4:30–32; Matt. 13:31–32; Luke 13:18–19; Gos. Thom. 84:26–33). These two parables will be seen in greater detail below.

Finally, discovery and joy predominate in the parables of the Lost Sheep (Matt. 18:12–13; Luke 15:4–6; Gos. Thom. 98:22–27) and the Lost Coin (Luke 15:8–9). It is interesting that the tradition has tended to interpret the Lost Sheep parable as telling how God and/or Jesus searches for the lost and the sinful, in other words, for us. So, ever since the framing of this parable within the interpretive verses of Luke 15:1–3, 7, the seeker is God and/or Jesus and we are the sought. No doubt it is hard ever to think otherwise after John 10:11, 14, had made Jesus announce: "I am the good shepherd." But the tradition never applied the same interpretation to the twin parable of the Lost Coin so that, God and/or Jesus being again the seeker, Jesus might be made to announce: "I am the good housewife." The reason is, I presume, obvious to all, but it does serve to cast doubt on the tradition's handling of the lost sheep. It would seem much better, however, to take the "joy" which accompanies the discovery of the treasure in Matt. 13:44 as the same "joy" which accompanies the finding of the lost sheep and the lost coin in Luke 15:5, 6, 9. These parables image what *we* must find even if it is true that it is a finding of that by which we were already and always found.

Two comments are necessary before we can proceed. In our present gospel texts there are fewer parables of advent than of reversal and fewer of these than of action. We have no way of knowing if this represents the emphasis of the historical Jesus but one would suspect that it does not. The parables in which Jesus expressed his experience of God's advent were quite unnecessary for a later tradition which itself experienced God in the cross and resurrection of Jesus. For them God's advent was not in harvest but in Christ. Most likely, then, the paucity of such parables reflects the tradition's needs and not Jesus' emphasis. Second, it must be understood that the interpretation offered here brackets completely the present interpretive settings of the parables within the gospel texts. This is not to say that such frames are wrong or useless. They pertain, however, to later layers of the tradition and should be bracketed in studying the historical Jesus.

The validity of this methodology must now be seen in detail for two of the parables of advent, the Sower and the Mustard Seed. For each parable we shall have to write a history of the sequential stages of its transmission, tracing the history of the tradition back to the earliest form of the story. When this is done for each one, some general conclusions on both can be drawn within the understanding of the parabolic intentionality of Jesus.

2. *The Sower*

There are four different texts of the parable: those in Matt. 13:3–8 and Luke 8:5–8 which, on the more usual source-critical hypothesis, are based on that of Mark 4:3–8, and an independent version in Gos. Thom. 82:3–13. The three Synoptic Gospels also contain a detailed allegorical interpretation in Mark 4:14–20, Matt. 13:19–23, and Luke 8:11–15, which is *not* present in the Gospel of Thomas. In effect, then, we shall be comparing only two independent versions in seeking the more original parable.

(1) The Synoptic Tradition. The text of the Markan version of this parable reads as follows. Typographical indications will be given to draw attention to certain points which will be under discussion.

(3) Listen! A sower went out to sow. (4) And as he sowed, SOME SEED fell along the path, and the birds came and devoured it. (5) OTHER SEED fell on rocky ground, where it had not much soil, and immediately it sprang up, *since it had no* [depth of soil; (6) and when the sun rose it was scorched, and *since it had no*] root it withered away. (7) OTHER SEED fell among thorns and the thorns grew up and choked it, and it yielded no grain. (8) And OTHER SEEDS fell into good soil and brought forth grain, [growing up and increasing] and yielding thirtyfold and sixtyfold and a hundredfold.

The major problem will be to determine if the Markan text shows any signs of expansion over a pre-Markan earlier version.

(a) The Parable. There are three major points to be noted concerning Mark's text: the expansions in 4:5–6 and 4:8 and the contrast of singular seed in 4:3–7 with the plural seeds in 4:8. They will be seen in this order.

There are five elements in the Markan parable: the opening in 4:3, the path in 4:4, the rocks in 4:5–6, the thorns in 4:7, and the good ground in 4:8. Attention is immediately drawn to the rocks in 4:5–6, for three reasons. First, it is a much longer section than any of the others, and significantly longer than even the final and climactic unit of the good ground. Second, there is a triple repetition of the lack of ground: not much soil, no depth of soil, no root. Third, and most important, two conflicting images are presented here. In 4:6a the picture is of seed that does not survive the first morning's scorching sun, but in 4:5, 6b, the image is of seed that grows for a while and then withers.

The reactions of Matt. 13:5–6 and Luke 8:6 to their Markan source are rather significant. Matthew sees no problem and accepts Mark's version, but Luke drastically revises it. He erases completely the triple redundancy concerning lack of soil to a single, "because it had no moisture." He solves the conflict of imagery by having the seed fall, "on the rock; and as it grew up, it withered away," thereby removing the problematic sun from the picture. Luke's literary instinct pruned the story back very close to its original pre-Markan version. This pre-Markan version would have read something like this: "Other seed fell on rocky ground, where it had not much soil, and immediately sprang up, [and] since it had no root it withered away." The addition of the sun in 4:6a caused certain textual dislocations which are rather important. The one who inserted this 4:6a used the phrase "since it had no . . ." as a frame for his insertion. He copied the idea of the lack of soil ("depth of soil") in 4:5b from the original lack ("not much soil") in 4:5a, and then put in his new 4:6a concerning the sun's scorching advent before repeating "since it had no . . ." and rejoining the original ending in 4:6b. We shall see this technique of framing an insertion again in the parable of the Mustard Seed and there it will be recognized as the hand of Mark himself.

There is a second expansion in 4:8, "growing up and increasing." This is a strange and somewhat belated way of specifying the already noted "brought forth grain." Both Matt. 13:8 and Luke 8:8 omit this phrase. The reasons for these two expansions, 4:6 and 4:8, will be discussed below.

There is one other aspect of the Markan text to be noted. The distinction between the wasted seed in 4:3–7 and the fruitful seed in 4:8 is stressed in Mark by two formal features. First, the seed is described as "some seed . . . other seed . . . other seed" in 4:3–7, but as "other seeds" in 4:8. There is thus a change from singular to plural between the units. Matt. 13:4, 5, 7, 8, pluralizes this consistently as "other seeds," and Luke 8:5, 6, 7, 8, singularizes it consistently as "some." But the Markan distinction of singular and plural might best be translated as "some . . . other . . . other . . . the others (=the rest)." Second, this distinction and contrast is underlined by the phrase "it yielded no grain" in Mark 4:7b which refers immediately to the seed among thorns but also reflects back on all the wasted seed in 4:3–7. As such it is in sharp juxtaposition with the fate of the fruitful seed which follows with "brought forth grain" in 4:8. The contrast is much clearer in the Greek where the same phrase is used in both cases and where the Semitic underlayer (literally: "gave fruit") is still quite visible. There is even a third formal feature of contrast in that three degrees of loss lead to three degrees of gain. All of this means that there is not an even emphasis on four situations (path, rocks, thorns, good ground), but a formal balance and contrast between three situations of waste and failure and three situations of gain and success.

(b) The Interpretation. This analysis presumes the basic accuracy of the modern claim that this interpretation of the Sower parable is from a later strand of the tradition and so does not derive from the historical Jesus himself. The arguments will only be summarized here. First, the parable exhibits rather heavily the characteristics of translation Greek from an Aramaic original. Second, the interpretation is in ordinary Greek and replete with the language and concepts of the primitive church. For the present purpose of writing a history of the parable's tradition back to Jesus, the interpretation is taken as inauthentic but it will be helpful to see if its presence has effected any changes in the parable itself. In other words, does the presence of the interpretation explain the expansions noted above in the parable? Did Mark make the changes in the parable with one eye on the interpretation?

The insertion of the sun in 4:6a with the attendant literary dislocations in 4:5–6 can be explained as an effect of the interpretation's presence within the situation of the Markan community. The one who inserted the sudden arrival of the scorching sun in 4:6a wished to underline most forcibly what the advent of "tribulation or persecution" in 4:16–17 was really like: not slow withering but instant scorching. It is interesting that Luke 8:13, having removed the sun in his 8:6, tones down his interpretation and mentions only "time of temptation": temptation withers, persecution scorches. So also the insertion in 4:8 can be understood as bringing parable and interpretation into relevant alignment for the necessities of Mark's community. They have to be warned not only of the fiery advent of persecution (so 4:6a) but also of the growth and perseverance which is necessary even for believers (so 4:8). The harvest of 4:8 is no instant and easy consummation but a slow process of growth. Or, as Mark 13:13 sums up both these insertions, "he who endures to the end will be saved." In other words, both insertions tend to emphasize certain aspects of the parable's interpretation needed for Mark's purpose, and as such, of course, they do not belong to the original parable of Jesus.

(2) The Gospel of Thomas. The narrative in Gos. Thom. 82:3–13 does not exhibit the anomalies noted above in Mark 4:5–6 on withering and scorching. In 82:6–8: "Others fell on the rock and did not strike root in the earth and did not produce ears." There is no mention at all of the sun's scorching advent, but the failure of root in earth is mentioned. So also in 82:11–12 the text has no equivalent to the mention of growth and increase in Mark 4:8. It states simply: "And others fell on the good earth and brought forth fruit." In both cases the pre-Markan text is close to that of the Gospel of Thomas.

But, on the other hand, Gos. Thom. 82:3–13 does not have the clear twofold contrast of lost seed and fruitful seed seen earlier in Mark 4:3–7 as against 4:8. It has the same fourfold division ("some . . . others . . . others . . . others") as in the other synoptics, and in the interpretation itself. This will have to be seen again later.

Another difference between Mark 4:8 and Gos. Thom. 82:11–13 concerns the yield of the harvest. The former has: "it brought forth good fruit; it bore sixty per measure and one hundred twenty per measure." First, as others also have noted, the interest in Mark 4:8 remains consistently on the seeds, as it was throughout: some ears yield as high as one hundred grains. But 82:11–13 shifts the focus to the yield of various parts of the field in comparison with the amounts therein sowed. Second, there is a threefold measure in Mark 4:8 (30, 60, 100) but a twofold one in 82:11–13 (60, 120).

(3) The Earliest Version. The most striking similarity between the versions of the Gospel of Thomas and Mark is in their paratactic construction and in their constant use of threefold structure. This shows up even in translation and can be indicated rather easily by noting the main verbs. For example, with regard to the seed near the path, Mark 4:4 has: "seed fell/birds came/ate it"; and Gos. Thom. 82:5–6 has: "fell/birds came/gathered them." It is not claimed that this triple-strophic construction can still be discovered in full detail but the general coincidence in form is still very striking. The first conclusion, then, is that the earliest version was very paratactic, using short terse sentences connected by simple "and." It also favored a threefold structure as much as possible.

The second conclusion derives immediately from this characteristic threefold structure. The triple ending of Mark 4:8 (30, 60, 100) is more original than the double ending of Gos. Thom. 82:13 (60, 120). Apart from reasons mentioned earlier, there is one more to be noted. The 60/120 of Thomas may be better mathematics than the 30/60/100 of Mark but it is not as good poetry. B. H. Smith has discussed the special problems of poetic closure especially for paratactic structures and concluded that "one of the most common and substantial sources of closural effects in poetry is the terminal modification of a formal principle." The constant use of threesomes is broken here by the terminal 100 (rather than 90 or 120) which is itself a number representing consummation and completeness. The parable is ended.

The third conclusion is probably the most important of all. This concerns the twofold distinction of three cases of loss and waste in Mark 4:3–7 as contrasted with three cases of gain and success in 4:8. In the other synoptics, in the allegorical interpretation, and in the Gospel of Thomas the emphasis is on four different situations. Which is more original? The version in Mark seems more authentic not only because of the repeated Semitism seen earlier in 4:7, 8, but because the fourfold division seems to have appeared under the influence of allegorical interpretation. The irony is that the interpretation is present in Mark 4:-14–20 and yet the parable has still retained its original formal balance in 4:3–8, while Gos. Thom. 82:3–13, which lacks any allegorical interpretation attendant on it, has still lost the original 3/3 comparison. One can presume, however, that even in the Gospel of Thomas the parable was read and understood as depicting the failures and successes of true gnosis. Once such an allegorical reading, however general and implicit, was introduced the careful literary balance and stylization of three losses versus three gains would soon become problematic. One might be able to see applications of the three degrees of loss but what was one to do with the three degrees of gain? The result was inevitable: the three degrees of gain become two in Gos. Thom. 82:13 and are reduced to one ("a hundredfold") in Luke 8:8. Hence the division in two threes (3/3) becomes a simple fourfold (1/2/3/4) one. This has not yet happened in Mark 4:3–8 despite the presence of the interpretation but it has happened in Thomas even without the explicit interpretation.

The conclusion is now ready. The original version of the Sower is best reflected in the pre-Markan text, that is, in Mark 4:3–8 without the insertions in 4:5–6 and 4:8. It was very paratactic and used to a consummate degree the folkloric threesome. It contrasted sharply three varying degrees of wasted seed (path, rocks, thorns) with three varying degrees of fruitful seed (30, 60, 100). This contrast was heightened by the longer description of the former cases and the terse but triumphant announcement of the latter ones. There is no evidence that the "threes" had any allegorical function. They represent a contrast rendered in poetic stylization. What this would have meant for Jesus will be seen after consideration of the Mustard Seed.

3. *The Mustard Seed*

Once again there are four versions of this parable. One is in Mark 4:30–32. Those in Matt. 13:31–32 and Luke 13:18–19 are based, in the more usual Two-Source hypothesis, on Mark 4:30–32 and also on the other written source common to Matthew and Luke and known to scholarship by the code-letter Q. This term rather graphically reflects its enigmatic status in criticism. This source is not known in any independent text but it can be reconstructed here by noting what is common to Matthew and Luke but not derived from Mark. Finally, there is a version of the parable in Gos. Thom. 84:26–33. In this case, therefore, we shall be comparing three independent versions: that in Mark, that in Q as reconstructed from Matthew and Luke, and that in the Gospel of Thomas.

(1) The Synoptic Tradition. The first step is to compare the two independent sources, Mark and Q, and this means that the content of Q must be established in the process.

(a) The Markan Version. Since the parable is so short it will be possible to give all three independent sources in full. To begin with Mark 4:30–32:

> (30) And he said, "With what can we compare the kingdom of God, or what parable shall we use for it? (31) It is like a grain of mustard seed, which, when sown upon the ground, is the smallest of all the seeds on earth; (32) yet when it is sown it grows up and becomes the greatest of all shrubs, and puts forth large branches, so that the birds of the air can make nests in its shade."

Sowing and Size. The grammar of Mark 4:31–32 is notoriously bad. This might be explained to a certain extent by postulating fairly literal translation from an Aramaic original. However, while Semitisms abound in all three seed parables in Mark 4, the Mustard Seed seems to have the worst Greek of them all. The question thus arises whether the difficulties in Mark 4:31–32 stem not only from translation Greek but also from Mark's editorial tampering with an earlier version of the parable. In order to see this possibility more clearly, 4:31–32a can be lined out as follows:

(a)   which, when sown
(b)   upon the ground,
(c)   is the smallest of all the seeds
(b')   on earth [literally in Greek: upon the ground];
(a')   yet when [it is] sown
(d)   it grows up and becomes
(c')   the greatest of all shrubs,
(e)   and puts forth large branches

Three things should be noted immediately: the redundancy in *abcb'a'* and the way in which *c* is framed by *ab* and *b'a'*; the balanced contrast in *c/c'*; and the rather anticlimactic note in *e* after the superlative comment in *c'*. These will be taken up separately in this order.

The redundancy which frames the phrase "is the smallest of all the seeds" in 4:31 is rather like the literary technique of redundant framing seen earlier for the Sower in Mark 4:5–6. J. R. Donahue has drawn attention recently to this "Markan insertion technique" whereby Mark makes an insertion into his source text and then repeats after it the phrase which preceded it. Two examples must suffice. The repetition of " 'Rise, take up your pallet' " in Mark 2:9b and 2:11 frames the Markan insertion of "But that you may know that the Son of man has authority on earth to forgive sins" in 2:10. So also the repetition of " 'Son of David, have mercy on me!' " in Mark 10:47b and 10:48b frames the Markan addition of "And many rebuked him, telling him to be silent; but he cried out all the more" in 10:48a. Most likely, then, the elements *ab* came from Mark's source but it is he himself who added in element *c* concerning the mustard seed as the smallest of all, and then repeated, in reversed order, the source's elements *b'a'*.

If *cb'a'* is a Markan redactional insert, it is also necessary to see *c'* as his own addition. The phrase in *c'*, "the greatest of all shrubs," is a clear parallel with the preceding *c*, "the smallest of all the seeds." In other words, the entire small*est*/larg*est* contrast in this superlative form is from Mark himself and not the original parable.

Finally, there is the description of the large branches in element *e*. If the superlative description of *c'* is a Markan insertion, then the phrase "and puts forth large branches" can stand quite well as the pre-Markan account of the final growth situation.

The Shaded Birds. Commentators usually remind us that the description of the birds nesting in the shady branches is an allusion to certain Old Testament texts such as Ps. 104:12 and/or Dan. 4:10–12 and/or Ezek. 17:23; 31:6. If one makes the mistake of actually looking up these references, one immediately senses a problem: the allusion is not very explicit and not very appropriate. The allusion, if present, is not an explicit citation of any presently known source, and, if it refers to all these places together, they form a rather strange unity. The image of nesting birds, but with no mention of a *tree*, appears literally as an example of God's loving care for nature in Ps. 104:12, "the birds of the air have their habitation; they sing among the branches." All the other uses are metaphorical, and here it is always a question of a tree, and indeed of a very, very great tree. So, for Nebuchadnezzar in Dan. 4:10–12, "I saw . . . a tree in the midst of the earth; and its height was great. The tree grew and became strong, and its top reached to heaven, and it was visible to the end of the whole earth . . . and the birds of the air dwelt in its branches." Later, in 4:20–21, Daniel explains that the great tree is the king himself. The image is used for Pharaoh of Egypt in Ezek. 31:3, 6: "I will liken you to a cedar in Lebanon . . . of great height, its top among the clouds. . . . All the birds of the air made their nests in its boughs." In Ezek. 17:23 the Messiah is envisaged as "a noble cedar . . . in the shade of its branches birds of every sort will nest."

Because of these texts the commentators usually see in the ending of the Mustard Seed parable a reference to apocalyptic eschatology and its image of the end-time as a great tree with birds nesting in its branches. But it must be noted that in Daniel and Ezekiel the references are to a great and mighty tree or to the majestic cedar of Lebanon, and that there is always the parallelism of nesting birds and resting beasts: the former are in the branches; the latter are in the shade of the tree. Only Ps. 104:12, which does not mention a *tree* at all and does not have this poetic parallelism of nesting birds and resting animals, would be a viable allusion for a parable concerning a mustard shrub which, as J. D. Kingsbury has noted, "cannot, by any stretch of imagination, be classified as a . . . tree proper."

This, then, is the crux of the problem. If one intended an image of the apocalyptic advent, the mighty cedar of Lebanon was ready at hand in the tradition. If one needed an image of growth to this advent, the figure of a cedar shoot planted on a high mountain was also in the tradition. The mustard seed can grow only into a bush or shrub and, at its very best, is hardly competition for the Lebanese cedar. When one starts a parable with a mustard seed one cannot end it with a tree, much less the great apocalyptic tree, unless, of course, one plans to lampoon rather rudely the whole apocalyptic tradition. In other words, *if* there is any Old Testament allusion behind the original version of Mark 4:31, it is no more and no less than an allusion to God's loving providence in the pastoral scene of Psalm 104:12.

(b) The Q Version. This must be reconstructed from those places where Matthew and Luke agree with each other but do not derive this agreement from Mark. The reconstruction is facilitated by the fact that, as B. H. Streeter stated long ago: "This overlapping of Mark and Q . . . whenever it occurs, we find that Luke tends to preserve the Q version unmixed, while Matthew combines it with that of Mark." We can give here the text of Luke 13:18–19 which is probably very close to the Q source itself:

He said therefore, "What is the kingdom of God like? And to what shall I compare it? (19) It is like a grain of mustard seed which a man took and sowed in his garden [Q: field?]; and it grew and became a tree, and the birds of the air made nests in its branches."

Sowing and Size. One can see, for example, the Q text's account of the sowing in the phrase "which a man took and sowed in his field," which is present in Matthew and Luke, as against the account of Mark, "which, when sown upon the ground." But, apart from such minor differences, the crucial point is that the Q text does not have the superlative contrast of smallest/greatest which we earlier argued came from Mark himself into his version. Superlative contrast is not original.

The Shaded Birds. It is also clear that the Q text ended with a mention of the nesting birds. Both Matthew and Luke follow its version of birds nesting in the branches rather than Mark's one of birds nesting in its shade. Actually, it would seem that the birds are attracted to the mustard shrub "by the shade and the seed," in the words of J. Jeremias, and that, as H. K. McArthur has said, "Even though the mustard plant grows to a height of 8 to 12 feet, and the birds do sit in its branches, it is questionable whether they actually build their nests there." Be that as it may, a more important point is that the Q text has already tried to bring the original parable of the mustard shrub into better alignment with the figure of the great apocalyptic tree of the Old Testament tradition noted earlier. In Q it said simply and flatly, "and it grew and became a tree," as in Luke 13:19. Matt. 13:32 tries a valiant conflation between Q and Mark and reads, "it is the greatest of shrubs and becomes a tree." An obvious tension is being created between an original parable which ended with a *shrub* and a desire to bring in the Old Testament tradition of the apocalyptic *tree.* But, once again, *if* there is any Old Testament reference behind the original parable, it could only have been Ps. 104:12.

(2) The Gospel of Thomas. The final version to be considered is that in Gos. Thom. 84:26–33. It read as follows:

The disciples said to Jesus: Tell us what the Kingdom of Heaven is like. He said to them: It is like a mustard-seed, smaller than all seeds. But when it falls on the tilled earth, it produces a large branch and becomes shelter for (the) birds of heaven.

It is significant that this version does not have the two specific problems of the Markan (smallest/greatest) and the Q (shrub/tree) texts. The contrast of initial smallness and terminal greatness is more exactly delineated as a progress from a seed "smaller than all seeds" to a "large branch."

The mention of the birds concerns "shelter" and says nothing of nests. It is thus even farther removed from any Old Testament references to the great apocalyptic tree than were Mark and Q. The image is of birds finding shade beneath the wide branches of the shrub, as, for example, in Ps. 104:12.

(3) The Earliest Version. This comparison between the Q text, the pre-Markan one, and that in Gos. Thom. 84:26–33 gives us a good idea of what the earliest version must have contained. The original image was a contrasting diptych of the proverbially small (smallest of all?) mustard seed and the large branches of the grown mustard shrub beneath which the birds can find shade. It was the attempt to allude to the tree with the nesting birds of apocalyptic eschatological imagery which created the internal tensions of shrub/tree in Q or smallest/largest in Mark. In this case Gos. Thom. 84:26–33 is much closer to the original, although even here the "tilled earth" is probably a gnostic admonition.

4. *Growth or Miracle?*

This chapter began with a quotation from Ezra Pound on the natural symbol. His admonition can be reiterated now in the words of another poet, Allen Tate: "The abstraction of the modern mind has obscured their way into the natural order. Nature offers to the symbolic poet clearly denotable objects in depth and in the round, which yield the analogies to the higher syntheses." We tend to think of sowing and harvesting, or of seed and shrub, in terms of organic growth and normal biological development. The biblical mind knew also about growth and development but, more importantly, it took very seriously the God who gave them both as gift. When one reads in Gen. 8:22, " 'While the earth remains, seedtime and harvest, cold and heat, summer and winter, day and night, shall not cease,' " it is clear that those four simple "ands" are seen as the gifts of One whose promise alone guarantees their regularity and inevitability. Harvest follows seedtime on the pledge of God never again to destroy their sequence as absolutely as had been done in the Flood at the time of Noah in Gen. 6—7.

All of this is graphically illustrated by Paul's use of the sowing image in 1 Cor. 15:35–44. He wishes to express a mystery of continuity and also a paradox of discontinuity between the body one has here on earth and the body one will have in heaven. This transformation is certainly no process of normal growth and development and yet he finds the best image for it is this: "What is sown is perishable, what is raised is imperishable. It is sown in dishonor, it is raised in glory. It is sown in weakness, it is raised in power. It is sown a physical body, it is raised a spiritual body." As Ernst Käsemann put it: "In places where we would speak of development, the idea of miracle takes hold in Paul, the miracle which bridges the gap between different things."

So it is with the parables of the Sower and the Mustard Seed. In both cases there are sharp juxtapositions of two states. In the Sower it is three instances of sowing losses but then three instances of harvest gains. In the Mustard Seed it is the small seed sown but the large shade of the plant. These should not be called, in the phrase of N. A. Dahl, "parables of growth." Of course there is growth present and of course the biblical mind was aware of such growth. But the diptych of juxtaposition does not wish to emphasize growth but miracle, not organic and biological development but the gift-like nature, the graciousness and the surprise of the ordinary, the advent of bountiful harvest despite the losses of sowing, the large shade despite the small seed. It is like this that the Kingdom is in advent. It is surprise and it is gift.

If we can borrow a parallel from a totally different linguistic and poetic world, that of the hokku or haiku, it may help us to understand this effect. Take, for example, the poem of Moritake, as cited by C. Brooke-Rose:

> The fallen blossom flies back to its branch:
> A butterfly.

Here we cannot think of organic growth and development and yet this "miracle" while biologically unlikely is rendered almost linguistically inevitable. One notes how the consonants of the first line (f,l,b) and its verb (flies) seduce one poetically into accepting the second line's magic: a butter*fly*. This miraculous juxtaposition of leaf/butterfly is poetically parallel to the contrasts in Jesus' parables between three sowing losses/three harvest gains and between small seed/large shade. In the haiku the long first line renders the terse juxtaposition of the second one especially striking. So also with the Sower. The long and detailed account of the three losses make the short description of the three gains peculiarly effective. We are being asked in these parables to enter into images of the Kingdom's advent taken from the gracious gift and perennial surprise of nature's inevitability. But, maybe, in the final analysis, it will be necessary for us to read much more of the poetry of Ted Roethke in order to understand these pastoral parables of Jesus.

One final point. In Hermann Hesse's novel *Siddhartha* there is a scene between Siddhartha and the Buddha. The latter has just finished a sermon replete with teachings and doctrines on how one should live. But there is one problem, as Siddhartha tells him: " 'To nobody, O Illustrious One, can you communicate in words and teachings what happened to you in the hour of your enlightenment. The teachings of the enlightened Buddha embrace much, they teach much—how to live righteously, how to avoid evil. But there is one thing that this clear, worthy instruction does not contain; it does not contain the secret of what the Illustrious One himself experienced—he alone among hundreds of thousands.' " It is one thing to communicate to others conclusions and admonitions based on one's own profound spiritual experience. It was this that Pharisaic theology did so admirably at the time of Jesus. It is quite another thing to try and communicate that experience itself, or, better, to assist people to find their own ultimate encounter. This is what Jesus' parables seek to do: to help others into their own experience of the Kingdom and to draw from that experience their own way of life.

three

PARABLES
OF REVERSAL

Therefore, see without looking, hear without listening, breathe
   without asking:
The Inevitable is what will seem to happen to you purely by chance;
The Real is what will strike you as really absurd;
Unless you are certain you are dreaming, it is certainly a dream of
   your own;
Unless you exclaim—"There must be some mistake"—you must be
   mistaken.

> (W. H. Auden, "For the Time Being")

Parables of advent would seem to be the most difficult to create. One
must forge images of mystery and surprise, and one must speak of what
comes beyond expectation or, even if expected, is always experienced as
permanently gracious and undeserved. Above all, the revelation must
articulate itself in forms and terms adequate to its experience. It is,
therefore, not unimportant that Jesus' parables of the Kingdom's advent
are taken from the utter normalcy of actual or possible existence. The
advent of the Kingdom is at once utterly awesome and awesomely
normal. One enters another world and a different Kingdom in the
images of the apocalyptic Revelation of John.

Giles Gunn has summed up very accurately the difficulties of expressing such parables of advent: "The names we so glibly attach to such
revelatory experiences suddenly grate upon the ear. Certain actions

53

which all at once seem inevitable and necessary fill familiar beliefs and former ideas to the bursting point with new and unforeseen meaning. Life suddenly releases some of its unspent force, and conventional expectations and interpretations are toppled by the flood of new insight and illumination." This last sentence serves as a good transition to those images of Jesus which are here termed "parables of reversal." In the programmatic parable of the Treasure, the man who found it "goes and sells all he has," according to Matt. 13:44, and thereby secures the field and its contents. The treasure's advent involves a complete ("all") overturning of his past and also, of course, a perfectly sensible and very willing abandonment of all he had previously held important up to that moment. One might object that the finding of hidden treasure is an utterly obvious cliché of folktales and that the selling of the finder's possessions and the abandonment of his past is an inevitable facet of any such story. It is interesting, therefore, to compare Jesus' parable with the rabbinical use of such a basic folkloric theme. It is given in the translation of J. D. Kingsbury:

To what is the matter like? To one who received a large field in a province of the sea (i.e. in the far distance, in the remote West) as inheritance. And he sold it for a trifle. And the buyer went there and dug it up and found in it treasures of silver and treasures of gold and precious stones and pearls. Then the seller began to choke himself [for anger]. This is what the Egyptians did; for they sent away and did not know what they sent away; for it is written, "And they said, 'What is this we have done, that we have let Israel go from serving us?' " (Exod. 14:5)

There are three major points of difference in the two usages. First, the rabbinical use is intended as an illustration of the biblical text in Exod. 14:5, and, as such, is best described as allegory. Knowing the biblical text, one can easily decode the story. Indeed, this is a perfect example of the basic difference between Jesus' parables and the rabbinical examples. Second, the emphasis is on the seller in the rabbinical story but on the finder in Jesus' parable. Finally, and most significantly, in the rabbinical one the finder discovered the treasure *after* having bought the field, and thus there was never even the possibility of his selling all his goods. In no way is this intended to denigrate the rabbinical story in favor of that of Jesus. It is simply to insist that they are doing radically different things: one illustrates a rather obvious text which would be quite clear even without it; the other incarnates the mystery of the Kingdom's advent.

Advent demands reversal, but a very specific type of reversal. Once again an example from the world of the hokku or haiku may be helpful. Hugh Kenner, discussing its influence on Ezra Pound, noted that its action, "depends on Aristotle's central plot device, *peripeteia*, or 'reversal of the situation':

> Fu I loved the high cloud and the hill,
> Alas, he died of alcohol."

This might be termed a single reversal, the tragic reversal of an individual human life: high/died and loved-hill/alcohol. But Jesus' parables of reversal are not single reversals and not even double or parallel reversals. They are what might be best termed polar reversals. If the last becomes first, we have the story of Joseph. If the first becomes last, we have the story of Job. But if the last becomes first *and* the first becomes last we have a polar reversal, a reversal of world as such. When the north pole becomes the south pole, and the south the north, a world is reversed and overturned and we find ourselves standing firmly on utter uncertainty. The parables of reversal intend to do precisely this to our security because such is the advent of the Kingdom. Or, as Paul might have put it, see if you can boast from the middle of an earthquake.

1. *Parables and Examples*

In his classification of figurative speech in the synoptic tradition, R. Bultmann distinguished among four cases. First, *"Metaphors . . .* shortened comparisons lacking the comparative word," as in Matt. 5:13. Second, *"similitudes . . .* distinguished from comparisons or figures only by the detail in which the figure is painted," as in Matt. 18:12–14. Third, "the *Parable . . .* gives as its picture not a typical condition or a typical, recurrent event, but some interesting particular situation," so Luke 16:1–7. Finally, *"Exemplary stories* have a striking formal relationship to parables . . . even if they have no figurative element at all . . . exemplary stories offer examples = models of right behavior." The following are classed in this last category: the Good Samaritan, the Rich

Fool, the Rich Man and Lazarus, the Pharisee and the Publican, and, as "the first part of an exemplary story," the Wedding Guest and the Proper Guests. These will all be seen in more detail in this chapter. But it must be noted, even in passing, that all these are found only in Luke.

There is an immediate and rather obvious problem. Of the four classes cited from Bultmann the first three are sharply distinguished from the last one. Metaphors, similitudes, and parables are all figurative speech and differ among themselves only in whether such language is terse or developed and is using a typical case or an individual situation. But exemplary stories, hereafter called simply examples, are essentially different in that, as Bultmann noted, they may "have no figurative element at all." They are stories of how one should or should not behave in certain situations and, while being also paradigmatic for analogous cases, these stories could be actually lived out in practice. This must be emphasized as it is the core of the problem of parables versus examples. When Jesus gave the Sower parable, for example, his first hearers and his modern readers would probably all agree on one thing: Jesus was not interested in agrarian reform in eastern Galilee. Whatever he might have meant, one is immediately certain that agriculture is *not* the point of the story. But when Jesus tells parables whose content is not some morally neutral activity such as sowing or harvesting but involves a morally significant action it may not be at all so clear if he is giving examples (act/do not act like this) or telling parables.

It will be argued in this chapter that the parables of reversal have been turned in almost all cases into examples precisely because of this ambiguity. It will also be clear that Luke is especially fond of this type of transformed parable. No doubt it appealed to his historicizing tendencies, to that magnificent creative gift of his which, for example, located the Ascension and Pentecost in time and place giving them a local habitation and a name that Christianity has never been able thereafter to forget. His acceptance of many of Jesus' reversal parables as actual examples of good and/or bad ethical action has probably preserved them for us where otherwise they might well have been lost to us forever. But in this chapter we are interested in the historical Jesus and not in the creative genius of Luke. Our purpose will be to show that such examples, found mostly in Luke alone, were originally parables of reversal, as defined above. We shall look at the most famous one, the Good Samaritan, in full detail, and then discuss the others somewhat more swiftly. In this analysis there are no parallel texts to help us write a history of the transmission, so we shall be concentrating on discrepancies between story and context or on dislocations within the story as it is changed from parable to example.

2. The Good Samaritan

The story is found only in Luke 10:30–37. A glance at some recent literature on the story confirms that the Good Samaritan is classified or at least interpreted as an example by many of the major books on the parables. J. Jeremias interprets it as meaning: "The example of the despised half-breed was intended to teach him that no human being was beyond the range of his charity. The law of love called him to be ready at any time to give his life for another's need." E. Linnemann explains: "The story certainly leaves no doubt that what really matters is to act as the Samaritan did . . . in the same simplicity . . . governed completely by the need of the man who confronts us." G. V. Jones interprets the Samaritan with: "The parable is not a pleasant tale about the Traveller Who Did His Good Deed: it is a damning indictment of social, racial, and religious superiority." He later describes it as "a memorable illustrative story," which "issues the challenge to decide between the life of involvement or non-involvement," so that a man "understands and does what is actually required of him in his situation." N. Perrin understands the parable as: "an 'exemplary story' and as such concerned to teach by example, in this instance the example of true neighbourliness . . . to teach that the crucial aspect of human relationships is response to the neighbour's need." Finally, D. O. Via notes: "The behavior and attitude sketched in The Good Samaritan and The Rich Fool (example stories) are not comparable to or analogous to what a man should do or avoid but are exactly what he should do or avoid." In this general consensus that the Samaritan is an example rather than a parable there is one striking exception. C. H. Dodd does not use the classification and never discusses any of the examples save for a passing reference to Augustine's allegorization of the parable and to certain threefold aspects in it.

(1) The Meaning for Luke. This consensus that the Good Samaritan is an example appears quite unassailable when the story is read with its

present overture of Luke 10:25–29 and its present culminating admonition in 10:37b, " 'Go, and do likewise.' " But does this contextual unity of 10:25–37 come from the editorial work of Luke himself, or from the creative activity of the pre-Lukan tradition, or from the original situation of the historical Jesus?

The thesis is that the present context of the Good Samaritan parable in 10:25–29 and 10:37 is not original and therefore cannot be used to interpret the meaning of the parable for Jesus. Two main arguments will be developed in support of this: the presence of the context but not the parable in Mark, and the divergent uses of the term "neighbor" in context and parable in Luke. The full unit is too long to be given here and the reader is referred to the biblical text throughout this exposition.

In attempting to separate the various layers of the complex in 10:25–37 four separate units can be considered: the question concerning eternal life in 10:25–28; the question regarding one's neighbor in 10:29; the parable of the Good Samaritan which must include at least all of 10:35; the conclusion with question in 10:36, answer in 10:37a, and final admonition in 10:37b. These can be examined in that order.

(a) 10:25–28. The question concerning eternal life in Luke is very similar to that regarding the greatest commandment in Mark 12:28–31 and Matt. 22:34–40. Their literary comparison would indicate that a question put to Jesus and leading up to a citation from Deut. 6:5, " 'You shall love the Lord your God with all your heart,' " and from Lev. 19:18, " 'You shall love your neighbor as yourself,' " was present in both Q and Mark and that, as seen earlier for the Mustard Seed parable, Matthew conflated the text of Q with that of Mark while Luke preferred the text of Q to that of Mark. The evidence can be summarized as follows. First, the common use of Q by Matthew and Luke explains the terms "lawyer . . . test . . . Teacher . . . in the law" in Matt. 22:35–36 and Luke 10:25–26. Second, the conflation of Q and Mark in Matthew and the choice of Q over Mark by Luke shows up clearly in a comparison of Mark 12:28=Matt. 22:35=Luke 10:25: Mark has "asked"; Luke (=Q) has "to put him to the test"; Matthew (=Q+Mark) has "asked . . . to test him." Third, following Q, Luke has the lawyer answer with the Old Testament citations and Jesus approve his reply, while Mark has Jesus answer with the quotations and the lawyer approve his solution; and in this Matthew follows Mark to the extent of having Jesus answer but gives no approval from the questioner. Finally, Luke accepts Q in that the question is: " 'what shall I do to inherit eternal life,' " in 10:25, and this opening question is recalled in the conclusion in 10:28, " 'do this, and you will live.' " Matthew, on the other hand, follows Mark in having the initial question concern, " 'which is the great commandment.' " This detailed literary analysis means only one thing. Luke 10:25–28 is continued smoothly by the second question in 10:29 into the parable of 10:30–37, but no such parable is present in Mark or Matthew. In other words, the context of the Lukan parable appears in Mark *without* the parable itself. Obviously the parable is not so intrinsically united with the previous unit as to be inseparable from it.

(b) 10:29. The second question picks up the "neighbor" which ended the preceding 10:25–28 and repeats it. The neighbor is still seen as the one *to whom* something is to be done, as the recipient not the giver of help: "But he, desiring to justify himself, said to Jesus, 'And who is my neighbor?' " The literary analysis of the previous 10:25–28 within the synoptic tradition serves to draw attention to the fact that there is no trace of this 10:29 in either Mark or Matthew. Mark does not know this second question and Matthew does not accept it from Q.

(c) 10:30–35. There is a logical inconsistency between the meaning of the term "neighbor" in 10:27, 29, and in 10:36 so that the parable of 10:30–35 which is located between these two frames is pulled in opposite directions. In 10:27, 29, the neighbor is he to whom love must be offered; in 10:36 the neighbor is the one who offers love and mercy to another's need. In other words, the prefixing of 10:27, 29, would indicate that the neighbor in the parable is the wounded man by the roadside; but the suffixing of 10:36 would mean that the neighbor is the Good Samaritan himself. In noting this discrepancy one does not deny that it could be explained as intending to stress that love, mercy, or being a neighbor are all two-way streets binding, for example, both wounded Jew and helpful Samaritan. The value of the discrepancy is that it indicates the possibility of some sort of literary combination of divergent sources and so may help to separate an earlier parable from a later context.

This divergent use of "neighbor" in a passive (one to whom help is offered) sense in 10:27, 29, and in an active (one who offers help) sense in 10:36 indicates that the unity of the complex is not that of an authentic and original dialogue between Jesus and a questioner in 10:-25–37. The parable of 10:30–35 would fit quite well with 10:28–29 showing that the neighbor is anyone in need; and it would also fit well with 10:36 indicating that the neighbor is the one who assists another's need; but it cannot go with both 10:27, 29, and 10:36 simultaneously. With which "application" does the parable go? In view of the fact that Luke 10:25–28 (=Q) was found also in Mark 12:28–31 and conflated therewith in Matt. 22:34–40, it seems best to conclude that the originally separate units were Luke 10:25–28(29) and 10:30–36(37) and that these were united because of their common theme of "neighbor" but with its opposite meanings not totally harmonized and so still bearing witness to the divergent pieces of tradition in use.

If Luke 10:25–28(29) and 10:30–36(37) were originally not united from the historical Jesus' situation, was their unification effected in the pre-Lukan tradition or in the redaction of Luke himself? To be more specific: was the combination of the two pericopes already present in Q and thence retained by Luke while being broken apart by Matthew? This latter possibility seems to be the best solution. The main argument, about which more later, is that the compositional unity of 10:25–37 has been accomplished with a careful regard for the stylistic peculiarities of the controversy dialogue of the rabbinical tradition and this seems far more likely to have happened in the pre-Lukan tradition than to be the redactional creation of Luke himself. Also, if the combination of 10:25–37 was already effected in Q it is quite easy to see why Luke would want to retain it because of his interest in Samaria and the Samaritans (see Luke 9:52; 17:11, 16; Acts 1:8; 8:1, 5, 9, 14, 25; 9:31; 15:3), while Matthew would have a positive reason to omit it. Matt. 10:5 alone has the injunction from Jesus: " 'enter no town of the Samaritans.' "

(d) 10:36–37. Where exactly did the original parable end? In the present text the conclusion involves a question in 10:36, its answer in 10:37a, and an admonition in 10:37b. From a formal and stylistic point of view there is no difficulty in a parable ending with a rhetorical question or even with a question and answer, although this latter usage may often represent traditional or redactional expansion. As R. Bultmann has noted: "some parables end with a question directed to the hearer . . . it is questionable on occasions when the similitude is given in a framework by the answer being provided in the text, whether the framework is as original as the similitude itself. Here the editorial work of the evangelists has to be taken account of, as is perfectly clear from Luke 10:36–37."

The question in 10:36, " 'Which of these three, do you think, proved neighbor to the man who fell among the robbers?' " would serve as an excellent conclusion for the original parable. It is a rhetorical question with the answer already inevitable. The change from this unanswered rhetorical question in 10:36 to the question-and-answer format in 10:36–37a is an obvious change as soon as the questioner became identified as an individual lawyer or scribe. This would argue that the original ending was 10:36.

The answer in 10:37a does not in any way change the content of the parable and would make no difference in interpretation even if it were original. But there is another formal argument which indicates most persuasively that all of 10:37 stems from the same creative moment when 10:25–28 was added to 10:30–36 by means of the connective 10:29. This arises from the formal stylistics of the controversy dialogue. R. Bultmann summed up the form as follows: "the *reply* to the attack follows more or less a set form, with special preference for the counterquestion or the metaphor, or even both together.... The typical form for an answer is the counter-question [which sometimes] is a detailed *parable*, sometimes ending with a question, or at any rate interrogatory in form." The structural unity and formal balance of 10:25–27 can be outlined as follows:

Question (lawyer):	10:25	10:29
Counter-question (Jesus):	10:26	*10:30–36*
Answer (lawyer):	10:27	10:37a
Counter-answer (Jesus):	10:28	10:37b

Whoever united the previously separate units of 10:25–28 and 10:30–36 did more than merely juxtapose them and rely on the word-linkage of the term "neighbor" in 10:27, 29, 36, to hold them together. This pre-Lukan redactor carefully developed the parable in 10:30–36 by the new frames of 10:29 and 10:37 so that the final result was a beautifully constructed double controversy dialogue: in each half the question leads immediately into the counter-question, either biblical or parabolic, and in each half the lawyer's answer receives Jesus' counter-answer of approval. The two halves of the new creation end with very similar injunctions to action from Jesus: "said to him, '. . . do' " (10:28=37b). Formally it is perfect, but materially there is always the divergent meaning of "neighbor" in 10:36.

In summary, then. This is not an authentic dialogue between a lawyer and Jesus in 10:25–37; neither is it two original controversy dialogues in 10:25–28 and 10:29–37 word-linked by "neighbor." A single controversy dialogue in 10:25–28 has been very carefully and skillfully expanded into a double one by taking the originally quite separate parable of 10:30–36 and framing it with 10:29 and 10:37. Most likely this was already done in the pre-Lukan tradition and was taken over by Luke from Q. Formal and stylistic harmony combined with material and conceptual disharmony have argued the conclusion: the parable of the Good Samaritan in 10:30–36 was originally independent of its present context and must be interpreted therefore apart from that later framework.

(2) The Meaning for Jesus. We have seen what the story meant as an example embedded in a double controversy dialogue. What would it have meant for Jesus when the text is no more and no less than Luke 10:30–36? In answering this question the emphasis will be on the structural development and narrative details of the parable itself.

(a) The Structure of the Narrative. The story can be set out as follows:

(a)	10:30a:	"a man . . . fell among robbers"
(b)	10:30b:	terse description of action of robbers
(c)	10:31:	"a priest . . . saw him . . . passed by on the other side"
	10:32:	"a Levite . . . saw him . . . passed by on the other side"
	10:33:	"a Samaritan . . . saw him . . . he had compassion"
(b')	10:34–35:	very long description of the action of the Samaritan
(a')	10:36:	"the man . . . fell among the robbers"

It may be indicative to note the word distribution even in the English translation: (a) 14 words; (b) 12; (c) 22, 19, 19; (b') 66; and (a') 17 words. In doing this no assertions are being made concerning mathematics or even chiastics. It is just a rather conscious, abstract, and wooden way of appreciating the unconscious and intuitive perfection of a poet's rhythm and a master's style. But even the numbers will be of importance in assessing original emphases.

The narrative comes to a first climax in the balanced reactions of (c) 10:31–33: priest and Levite/*saw*/passed by on the other side, but the Samaritan/*saw*/had compassion. The second and final climax is the rhetorical question in 10:36. Once again, as in 10:31–33, the three are in question but now the emphasis has shifted from clerics versus Samaritan to hearer(s) versus Samaritan with: " 'Which of these three, do *you* think, proved *neighbor* . . . ?' " In literary sequence the robbers recede into the background, the clerics follow them into stylistic oblivion, and in 10:36 the hearer(s) has only one person left to face, and to face by one's own necessary decision: the Samaritan judged as good. It is at this point that the amount of space given to the description of the Samaritan's action in (b') 10:34–35 becomes significant. It reads: "and went to him and bound up his wounds, pouring on oil and wine; then he set him on his own beast, and brought him to an inn, and took care of him. And the next day he took out two denarii and gave them to the innkeeper, saying, 'Take care of him; and whatever more you spend, I will repay you when I come back.' " As noted earlier, even in English translation, far more space (66 words) is devoted to this description than to any of the other elements in the story. Why? When the hearer is confronted with the rhetorical question in 10:36 he might negate the entire process by simply denying that *any* Samaritan would so act. So, before the question can be put, the hearer must see, feel, and hear the goodness of the Samaritan for himself. The function of 10:34–35 and its detailed description is so to involve the hearer in the activity that the objection is stifled at birth. He has just seen a Samaritan do such a good action in very exact detail.

(b) The Importance of "Samaritan." It would be difficult to emphasize this point too much. Priests, Levites, and Samaritans have absolutely no emotional sociological overtones for the modern reader and yet, as has just been seen, it is important that it is precisely a "Samaritan" as such who performs the good deed. If Jesus wanted to teach love of neighbor in distress, it would have sufficed to use the standard folkloric threesome and talk of one person, a second person, and a third person. If he wanted to do this and add in a jibe against the clerical circles of Jerusalem, it would have been quite enough to have mentioned priest, Levite, and let the third person be a Jewish lay-person. Most importantly, if he wanted to inculcate love of one's enemies, it would have been radical enough to have a Jewish person stop and assist a wounded

Samaritan. But when the story is read as one told by the Jewish Jesus
to a Jewish audience, and presumably in a Jerusalem setting, this original
historical context demands that the "Samaritan" be intended and heard
as the socio-religious outcast which he was. As John 4:9 put it laconically:
"For Jews have no dealings with Samaritans." Hence the internal structure of the story and the historical setting of Jesus' time agree that the
literal point of the story challenges the hearer to put together two
impossible and contradictory words for the same person: "Samaritan"
(10:33) and "neighbor" (10:36). The whole thrust of the story demands
that one say what cannot be said, what is a contradiction in terms: Good
+Samaritan. On the lips of the historical Jesus the story demands that
the hearer respond by saying the contradictory, the impossible, the
unspeakable. The point is not that one should help the neighbor in need.
In such an intention the naming of the helper as a Samaritan before a
Jewish audience would be unnecessary, distracting, and, in the final
analysis, inimical and counterproductive. For such a purpose it would
have been far better to have made the wounded man a Samaritan and
the helper a Jewish man outside clerical circles. But when good (clerics)
and bad (Samaritan) become, respectively, bad and good, a world is
being challenged and we are faced with polar reversal.

(c) From Parable to Example. It is easy to see how the tradition
managed to change a parable into an example. Indeed, as the gospel
moved out into a Gentile environment where terms like "Samaritan"
had no meaning, it was probably even inevitable. One knows that in
parables there is, to put it very simply, a literal level and a metaphorical
level. There is a literal point which stems from the surface level of the
story, and a metaphorical one which lives on a much deeper level and
appears in a mysterious dialectic with the former point. In distinction
to this, of course, example has only one, literal level. This distinction of
two points is usually clear and noncontroversial in most of the parables
of Jesus. Take, for example, the parable of the Wheat and the Darnel
in Matt. 13:24–30. Imagine a hearer of Jesus nodding his head in
agreement that here was a wise man and that he himself had just learned
what to do if ever he found himself in such an agricultural crisis. Our
judgment would be immediate: he has missed the point completely; or,
more precisely, he has mistaken the literal point for the metaphorical
point. Even those who might never be able to agree on what this

metaphorical teaching actually is would agree that he erred in taking only this literal, even if very true and highly practical, application.

When we move from the "amoral" world of agriculture into parables which present "moral" actions, the danger of confusing the literal and metaphorical is greatly increased. If the protagonist is presented in a downright immoral action, confusion ensues, but at least the distinction between literal and metaphorical is usually maintained. The classic example of this confusion is, of course, the parable of the Unjust Steward in Luke 16:1–7. But, whatever the tradition's scandal, one is still sure that Jesus is not giving here an example of fiscal and administrative responsibility. But all of this becomes even more distressingly easy to do when the major protagonist of a parable is performing a *morally good* action on the literal level. In this case it is very simple to remain on this level and convert the parable into example. This is exactly what has happened to the Good Samaritan in the course of its transmission.

None of this denies in any way that what the Samaritan does is a good action absolutely to be imitated. The emphasis is, however, on the doer not the deed. The deed is good but, of course, the Old Testament presented examples of behavior just as good. There is one case of even better behavior, since it is mercy and kindness shown to beaten attackers, told in 2 Chron. 28:9–15. Jesus may even have had this case in mind when constructing his own parable. It concludes in 28:15 with the people of Samaria acting rather like the Samaritan: "[they] took the captives, and with the spoil they clothed all that were naked among them; they clothed them, gave them sandals, provided them with food and drink, and anointed them; and carrying all the feeble among them on asses, they brought them to their kinsfolk at Jericho."

If we abandon finally and completely the idea of an example, as deriving from the tradition and not from Jesus, we must see this as a parable and so suggest the leap from the literal point to the metaphorical point which is the real purpose of the literary creation. The literal point confronted the hearers with the necessity of saying the impossible and having their world turned upside down and radically questioned in its presuppositions. The metaphorical point is that *just so* does the Kingdom of God break abruptly into human consciousness and demand the overturn of prior values, closed options, set judgments, and established conclusions. But the full force of the parabolic challenge is that the *just so* of the metaphorical level is not ontologically distinct from the presence of the literal point. The hearer struggling with the contradictory dualism of Good/Samaritan is actually experiencing in and through this the inbreaking of the Kingdom. Not only does it happen like this, it happens in this. The original parabolic point was the reversal caused by the advent of the Kingdom in and through the challenge to utter the unutterable and to admit thereby that other world which was at that very moment placing their own under radical judgment.

3. *Other Reversal Parables*

The parable of the Good Samaritan has been studied in some detail as it is a paradigmatic case of parable transformed by the tradition into example. The other reversal parables will be seen in more summary fashion. These include all the examples in Bultmann's classification except the Rich Fool, which is a parable of action. One very striking parable of reversal, that of the Vineyard Workers in Matt. 20:1–13, will have to be postponed for later study in the next chapter.

(1) The Rich Man and Lazarus. The parable is found only in Luke 16:19–31 within the carefully formed literary unity of 16:1–31. This contains three main units. First, there are the frames formed by the parables of the Unjust Steward beginning with " 'There was a rich man . . .' " in 16:1–7, and of the Rich Man and Lazarus likewise starting with " 'There was a rich man . . .' " in 16:19–31. Second, the collection of sayings in between in 16:8–18 which are initially interpretive of 16:1–7, but eventually seem word-linked or theme-linked to one another. Third, there is the overall context which stresses the proper use of material goods, from the Unjust Steward who does it by alms in 16:9 (!) to the Rich Man who fails to help poor Lazarus.

Whatever may be the redactional activity of Luke himself in all this it is clear that the positioning of 16:19–31 within this larger literary complex places the emphasis on the proper use of worldly goods and on the failure of the rich man to do so. But if 16:19–31 is isolated from this context furnished by the tradition and the focus is placed on its own internal content, what could such a story have meant for the historical Jesus?

The concluding section in 16:27–31 concerning the resurrection can hardly be accepted as originally authentic if the principle of dissimilarity be taken at all seriously. There are too many links between this discussion of the "resurrection" of the rich man and that concerning Jesus' own resurrection in Luke 24 to be coincidence. Therefore, 16:27–31 must be taken as stemming from the early church rather than the historical Jesus. Four links can be specified. First, there is the theme of disbelief before the resurrected one in 16:31, "neither will they be convinced if some one should rise from the dead," and in 24:11, 25, 41, "they did not believe them. . . . 'O foolish men, and slow of heart to believe'. . . . And while they still disbelieved." Second, there is the double mention of Moses and the prophets in 16:29, 31, and in 24:27, 44. Third, the resurrected one is mentioned in 16:31, "one should rise from the dead," and in 24:46, "on the third day rise from the dead." Finally, the use of "they will repent" in 16:30 will reappear in Acts 2:38; 3:19; 8:22; 17:30; and 26:20 in kerygmatic contexts. Methodologically, Luke 16:27–31 cannot be taken as part of the original parable of Jesus. Most likely it is pre-Lukan and is a post-resurrectional application of the parable. It allegorically alludes to the Jewish refusal to accept either Moses or the prophets as witnesses to the resurrection of Jesus or even to accept the risen Jesus himself. When one reads 16:31, "He said to them, 'If they do not hear Moses and the prophets, neither will they be convinced if some one should rise from the dead,' " in its present context one thinks of Jesus and not the rich man.

It has already been established in scholarship that the story of situational reversal in 16:9–26 has basic affinities with folkloric materials in both Egyptian and Jewish tradition. But what appears clearly in both the Egyptian tale of Si-Osiris and the Jewish one concerning the poor scholar and the rich publican Bar Ma'jan is the *moral* judgment which explains the situational reversal. J. Jeremias has cited the conclusion of the Egyptian version: "He who has been good on earth, will be blessed in the kingdom of the dead, and he who has been evil on earth, will suffer in the kingdom of the dead." The titles of scholar and publican carry their own immediate moral overtones in the Jewish account. What is striking, especially against this background, is Jesus' omission of any moral preparation for the reversal or any ethical judgment on the earthly status of the participants. In a situation where riches were often construed as God's approval, and sickness often understood as God's curse or punishment, it cannot be immediately presumed that 16:19–26, as told here, would automatically beget moral judgment for Lazarus and against the rich man.

It seems best, then, to take 16:19–26 as an actual parable of Jesus. Its literal point was a strikingly *amoral* description of situational reversal between the rich man and Lazarus. Its metaphorical point was the reversal of expectation and situation, of value and judgment, which is the concomitant of the Kingdom's advent. As the judgments which have to be made on the clerics as against the Samaritan are forcibly reversed, so also those which might be expected concerning the sick beggar and rich man are turned upside down. Jesus was not interested in moral admonition on the dangers of riches—the folktale had already done this quite admirably—but in the reversal of human situation in which the Kingdom's disruptive advent could be metaphorically portrayed and linguistically made present.

(2) The Pharisee and the Publican. The parable is present only in Luke 18:10–14. It receives a clear interpretation in the opening 18:9: "He also told this parable to some who trusted in themselves that they were righteous and despised others." When the phrase "trusted in themselves" is compared with the phrase of Paul in 2 Cor. 1:9 concerning his sufferings, "but that was to make us rely not on ourselves," it takes on much more serious overtones. For the phrase in Paul, which is the same Greek as that in Luke, means satanic pride where trust in self is opposed to trust in God: "not on ourselves but on God who raises the dead." But if the prologue in 18:9 hints at satanic pride (man against God), this is hardly evident in the story which follows in 18:10–14 (man against man).

The Pharisee has gone up to the Temple, to pray, by thanking God. He may certainly be indicted for human pride and for exalting himself over the publican, but this is a long way from satanic pride and exalting oneself over God. Accordingly, the application in 18:9 does not fit with the parable in 18:10–14 but is an application of it. Likewise, the concluding comment in 18:14b, "For everyone who exalts himself will be humbled, but the man who humbles himself will be exalted," appears elsewhere as an independent saying of Jesus in Matt. 23:12 and Luke 14:11. It announces eschatological judgment by God (note the passives) and this is somewhat redundant and even a little contradictory to the divine judgment just recorded in 18:14a. The parable must be isolated from its present frames of both 18:9 and 14b and seen as an independent unit in 18:10–14a. If these are removed the narrative tells of a Pharisee who prays exactly according to the approved way of the time as both Qumran and the Talmudic tradition bear witness. And, on the other hand, the publican is not even as clearly repentent as is the one in Luke 19:1–10.

The literal point of the parable is a startling story of situational reversal in which the virtuous Pharisee is rejected by God and the sinful publican gains approval. The metaphorical challenge is again clear: the complete, radical, polar reversal of accepted human judgment, even or especially of religious judgment, whereby the Kingdom forces its way into human awareness. What, in other words, if God does not play the game by our rules?

(3) The Wedding Guest. In Luke 14:1–24 there is an evident literary unity in which various pieces involving the theme of a banquet are placed together in a banquet situation during the life of Jesus. First, there is the healing at a banquet on the Sabbath in 14:1–6. Second, the parable of the Wedding Guest in 14:7–11. Third, a lesson is given to the host concerning meals in 14:12–14. Fourth, the saying concerning the eschatological banquet in 14:15. Finally, there is the parable of the Great Supper in 14:16–24. The literary situation is as elegant as it is artificial, so that the parable in 14:8–11 has been smoothed into its present place by the application to Jesus' fellow guests in 14:7 although there is no evidence that their taking of the first places created any problems in the "actual" situation of the meal where Jesus was present. The parable, opened by 14:7, concludes with 14:11 concerning the reversal of the exalted and the humble which, as already seen, involves the eschatological judgment of God.

The injunction contained in 14:8–10 does not fit particularly well with its opening application and neither does it go well with its concluding 14:11. In itself it has to do with table etiquette and its motivation could be described at its most positive as utterly banal and at its most negative as rather immoral. One is told to take low seats at a banquet in order to be moved up higher and obtain glory before one's fellow guests. If one jumps immediately from earthy table etiquette to eschatological rewards, it may be possible to accept the parable as it stands. As one might humble oneself on earth to obtain earthly glory, so should one humble oneself on earth to obtain heavenly glory. This is possible but not totally convincing. Another interpretation can be offered which is close to the meaning of the other parables just seen. In 14:8–10 the literal point is a somewhat amusing everyday experience in which one can easily imagine a situation of polar reversal. Jesus is saying in effect: can you imagine a situation in which a man in first place ends up in last and vice versa? The story tells of the quite convincing possibility of a man who takes the first seat at a banquet, others arrive and take the intermediate seats, so that when a guest of great distinction arrives the first person must not only give up his first place but take the lowest. This example of situational reversal shows how the Kingdom arrives so that one experiences God's rule as that which turns one's world upside down and radically reverses its normalcy. The Kingdom is not one's ultimate concern but that which undermines one's ultimate concern.

(4) The Proper Guests. The admonition of Luke 14:12–14 appears only in Luke and, as just seen, it is part of the artificial literary unity of 14:1–24. It reads: "He said also to the man who had invited him, 'When you give a dinner or a banquet, do not invite your friends or your brothers or your kinsmen or rich neighbors, lest they also invite you in return, and you be repaid. But when you give a feast, invite the poor, the maimed, the lame, the blind, and you will be blessed, because they cannot repay you.' " This is not a parable and it is not even an example. It does not say "do likewise" but "do this." R. Bultmann has already noted that while this could "be the first part of an exemplary story" it is really "but [a] somewhat expanded warning[s]." It is included here, however, because of its importance for the succeeding parable in Luke 14:16–24 to which we can now turn.

(5) The Great Supper. There are three versions of this parable. The synoptic tradition is represented by Matt. 22:1–10 and Luke 14:16–24, and there is also a version in Gos. Thom. 92:10–35.

(a) The Synoptic Tradition. It is difficult to decide for sure whether Matthew and Luke both found this parable in Q or whether it belongs to their special and independent sources. The main difficulty is that Matthew's version has been considerably changed as compared with Luke's. He has made two major additions. First, he has added on at the end the originally independent parable of the Wedding Garment in 22:11–13 and then made some minor adjustments within the Great

Supper in preparation for this appendix. One realizes immediately that this inclusion breaks the logical unity of the parable. The host has just gathered guests off the streets without any warning in 22:9–10 and yet he now expects instant wedding garments and sartorial elegance in 22:11–13.

Second, Matthew has deliberately inserted allusions to the immediately preceding parable of the Wicked Husbandmen from 21:33–46 into the parable of the Great Supper. In this former parable, which will be seen in great detail in the next chapter, the evil tenants killed the owner's servants and even his son so that the owner came and "put those wretches to a miserable death" in 21:41. In the parable of the Great Supper, Matthew drew a parallel to this. The invited guests "seized his servants, treated them shamefully, and killed them. The king was angry, and he sent his troops and destroyed those murderers and burned their city." It is obvious that 22:6–7, just cited, could not have been part of the original parable: why such violence in declining a dinner invitation, and are we really to imagine the sending of a punitive expedition while the dinner grows cold on the table? Matthew's purpose is clear in all this. He has allegorized the parable into an image of the history of salvation, as he sees it, and by his addition of 22:11–13 he has actualized it in application to the internal tensions within the Matthean community. Those originally invited did not come (Israel) and so others (the Gentiles) were brought in to the banquet, but they must still be worthy of this invitation (problem people in Matthew's community). In other words, Matthew combined and collated three independent parables, the Wicked Husbandmen, the Great Supper, and the Wedding Garment into what R. J. Dillon called "the parables of the true Israel," a diptych allegorization of salvation history.

Luke's version may also represent incipient allegorization but it is certainly not as heavy-handed as Matthew's. For example, the double sending of the servants in 14:21, " 'Go out quickly to the streets and lanes of the city,' " and in 14:23, " 'Go out to the highways and hedges,' " may well represent the mission to Israel and to the Gentiles. Be that as it may, what Luke has certainly done is to moralize the parable. In 14:21 it is precisely "the poor and maimed and blind and lame" who are to be invited. This repeats, of course, the injunction of Jesus just seen in Luke 14:13, " 'But when you give a feast, invite the poor, the maimed, the lame, the blind.' " But the discrepancy is surely just as obvious so that the moralizing does not really work. Jesus said in 14:12–14 *not* to invite the rich but to invite the poor in order to be rewarded by God not man. The parable, on the other hand, tells a story in which the rich are first invited, decline the invitation, and the poor are then invited in second place. The point is not quite the same. In summary, the basic parable has been allegorized by Matthew into an image of the history of salvation and has been moralized by Luke into an example of rather doubtful ethical greatness.

(b) The Gospel of Thomas. Apart from the specific problems just noted in Matthew and Luke, there is one common problem in them both. The story presumes that the guests knew in advance the date of the banquet and that the servants are sent out to inform the guests that all is now ready. So Matt. 22:3, "sent his servants to call those who were invited," and Luke 14:16–17, "invited many; and at the time for the banquet he sent his servant to say to those who had been invited, 'Come; for all is now ready.' " This makes their refusal *at this time* quite inexplicable and their refusals and excuses become rather facetious. This increases their culpability and fits very well with the allegorization process as an attack on Israel which had long been invited and balked at the very moment of the banquet.

None of these problems are present in the Gospel of Thomas. There it seems that the host has suddenly decided on a banquet and sends out his servants while all things are in preparation: "A man had guest-friends, and when he had prepared the dinner, he sent his servant to invite the guest-friends. He went to the first, he said to him: 'My master invites thee.' " We are asked to imagine a host who rather imprudently plans a sudden dinner, starts the preparation, and sends out the sudden invitations for that very day. It is an utterly possible situation. One's sudden decision for a dinner finds one's chosen friends all busy. What to do with the already prepared food? There is absolutely no allegorization in this version. There would seem, however, to be a deliberate moralization of the parable, and, indeed, a more convincing one than Luke's. In Gos. Thom. 92:13–29 there are four refusals instead of the folkloric threesome in the synoptic tradition. The conclusion in 92:-34–35 is, "Tradesmen and merchants [shall] not [enter] the places of my Father." This may be a possible allusion to Zech. 14:21, "And there

shall no longer be a trader in the house of the Lord of hosts on that day,"
but it serves primarily as a moral condemnation of the invited guests
even if an externally appended one. In this context the parable is a
negative example concerning those first invited. It is a warning not to
let material cares distract one from the invitation to true gnosis. But is
is also clear that there is no trace of Luke's positive moral, no mention
of the poor. The injunction is simple: "The master said to his servant:
'Go out to the roads, bring those whom thou shalt find, so that they may
dine,' " in 92:31–34.

(c) The Earliest Version. If we leave aside, as we must, both the
allegorization by Matthew and the moralization, be it positive in Luke
concerning the invitation for the poor or negative in the Gospel of
Thomas concerning the failure of the rich, we are left with a very simple
and extremely possible story of situational reversal. A man decides on
a sudden dinner that very day and sends out his servant to his friends
as the dinner is being prepared. Because of the lack of warning each one
finds he has a perfectly reasonable excuse. But the result is a meal
prepared and a table empty. The host's reaction is to send the servant
out to get anyone he can. There is no implication that he is looking for
riffraff. But one can appreciate the host's anger, probably as much with
himself as with his friends. Can you imagine, asks Jesus, a situation in
which all the invited guests are absent from a banquet and all the
uninvited ones are present? This is fundamentally amoral and invites the
hearers to recognize a situation of total reversal: the invited are absent,
the uninvited are present. As parable it provokes their response to the
Kingdom's arrival as radical and absolute reversal of their closed human
situation.

(5) The Prodigal Son. Once again we have a parable which is found
only in Luke 15:11–32. In the light of the preceding two parables just
studied the original intention of this one becomes much clearer. It
might even be termed a variation on the banquet theme which Jesus
used in these two cases to imagine scenes of situational reversal: the first
last and the last first or the invited absent and the uninvited present.

As the parable now stands it forms part of a harmonious literary unity
in Luke 15:1–32. This is composed of three parables, the Lost Sheep,
the Lost Coin, and the Prodigal (Lost) Son. The introduction in 15:1–2
reads: "Now the tax collectors and sinners were all drawing near to hear

him. And the Pharisees and the scribes murmured, saying, 'This man receives sinners and eats with them.' " This renders the unified understanding of the three parables quite clear. Jesus, in the name of God, is receiving sinners because they are the lost ones (sheep, coin, son). So, on the other hand, the Pharisees and the scribes are like the elder brother in the parable of the Prodigal Son. We have already seen, however, that the seeker of the lost sheep and the lost coin is *not* Jesus and/or God but the one who is open to and seeking for the Kingdom's advent. The tradition admitted as much by being ready to accept Jesus as the Good Shepherd but not quite ready to have him as the Good Housewife. In other words, as already seen for Luke 14 and Luke 16, so here also in Luke 15 we are dealing with the tradition's literary combinations and interpretations. We must study the parable of the Prodigal Son apart from the interpretive introduction in 15:1–2.

In itself the parable indicates the double elements of the polar reversal with the sharpest formal clarity so far. After the opening in 15:11, "There was a man who had two sons," the parable falls into two halves. The first concerns "the younger of them" from 15:12 to the concluding phrase "make merry; for this my son was dead, and is alive again; he was lost, and is found" in 15:24a. The second half begins with "his elder son" in 15:25 and concludes with "make merry . . . for this your brother was dead, and is alive; he was lost, and is found" in 15:32. One notices the same wording at the end of the two parts in 15:24, 32. The story is utterly believable and quite possible. Can you imagine, asks Jesus, a vagabond and wastrel son being feted by his father and a dutiful and obedient son left outside in the cold? The story has not been loaded on either side, and it is left untold whether the elder son finally relents and goes inside after the father comes out to entreat him. One feels understanding for the position of all three protagonists, but in the end the parable shows a prodigal son inside feasting and a dutiful son ouside pouting.

J. Jeremias has interpreted this parable, as cited in the epigraph of this book, as being Jesus' defense of his association with the outcasts against the protests of the Pharisees. But this would seem to confuse cause and effect. The parable is cause and not effect of Jesus' life and action. Parables and analogies are notoriously weak in converting or convincing those who are not open to their vision or are clearly opposed to their purpose, but they are just as notoriously persuasive for those who are at least open to their challenge. As Ezra Pound put it: "You can PROVE nothing by analogy. The analogy is either range-finding or fumble. Written down as a lurch towards proof, or at worst elaborated in that aim, it leads mainly to useless argument, BUT a man whose wit teems with analogies will often 'twig' that something is wrong long before he knows why. Aristotle had something of this sort in mind when he wrote 'apt use of metaphor indicating a swift perception of relations.' " As long as Aristotle has been mentioned, it may be useful to give in more detail and in another translation the text to which Ezra Pound is referring: "But the greatest thing by far is to be a master of metaphor. It is the one thing that cannot be learnt from others; it is also a sign of genius, since a good metaphor implies an intuitive perception of the similarity of dissimilars." A bow from Greece to Galilee.

4. *Eschaton and Paradox*

The six parables just examined all portray metaphorically the polar reversal which the Kingdom's advent demands. If one uses the terms "good" and "bad" but taken rather in an ontological than an ethical sense, one can summarize their challenge as follows:

	GOOD ⟷	BAD
(1)	Priest & Levite	Samaritan
(2)	Rich Man	Lazarus
(3)	Pharisee	Publican
(4)	First-seated	Last-seated
(5)	Invited Guests	Uninvited Guests
(6)	Dutiful Son	Prodigal Son

Such double and opposite reversal is the challenge the Kingdom brings to the complacent normalcy of one's accepted world.

In recent scholarship this aspect of heightened paradoxicality has been noted in another area of Jesus' language. This is his use of proverbial sayings within the tradition of Israel's wisdom literature. In this case he might be described as moving strands of wisdom tradition into conjunction with prophetic and away from apocalyptic eschatology.

Although W. A. Beardslee was not speaking of the historical Jesus as such, he has drawn attention to the fact that among the proverbs of Jesus in the Synoptic Gospels there are many aphoristic sayings where the "paradox of intensified antithesis is putting pressure on the very presuppositions on which the clusters of wisdom-insights had been gathered together." It is also interesting, as he has said elsewhere and later, that "many of the most strikingly hyperbolic and paradoxical sayings of the Synoptic tradition are simply missing from Thomas." When these observations on proverb are placed beside the present parables of reversal, we are dealing with what N. Perrin has described as a "shattering of the categories established by our milieu research." This is only to be expected, of course, if such a shattering was the original intention of the historical Jesus toward his own milieu. What we are dealing with is the *formal* eschatology of Jesus' language. He announces God as the shatterer of world, as the One of permanent eschatology, and so his language is sharpened necessarily into paradox, for paradox is to language as eschaton is to world.

In discussing the conjunction of form and content in Pascal's *Pensées*, Lucien Goldmann commented: "For Pascal's message is that Man is great in that he searches for absolute values but small in that, without ever ceasing to search, he knows that he can never approach these values. The only form to express this content is, of course, one which does not prove the contrary; which doesn't show either a man who has abandoned the search or one who has approached the goal. The fragment is such a form." So also with Jesus. Paradox is the form of eschaton.

At this point a parallel from the linguisticality of a totally different religious experience may be helpful. Take two examples from the language of Zen Buddhism. W. Barrett has given the following example: "Or when another Master remarks on the difficulty of solving one of the Zen questions—which is equivalent to answering the riddle of existence itself—he does not merely say that it is difficult or so very very difficult that it is well-nigh impossible, but this: 'It is like a mosquito trying to bite into an iron bull.' The image lives because the image suggests the meaning beyond conceptualization." One recalls the saying of Jesus in Mark 10:25 concerning the shattering of personal world necessary for the rich man to accept the Kingdom: "It is easier for the camel to go through the eye of a needle than for a rich man to enter the kingdom of God." These two aphorisms are alike both functionally, conceptually, and even formally: small/large; animate/inanimate.

A second example. There is a Zen saying cited by Paul Reps: "Basho said to his disciple: 'When you have a staff, I will give it to you. If you have no staff, I will take it away from you.' " There is a very remarkable proverb of Jesus which appears in Mark 4:25 (=Matt. 13:12=Luke 8:18), in Q, whence Matt. 25:29=Luke 19:26, and also in Gos. Thom. 88:16–18. The text of Mark 4:25 reads: "For to him who has will more be given; and from him who has not [even what he has] will be taken away." The part placed here in parentheses breaks the otherwise perfect parallelism of the aphorism and may even be a first, and not too success-ful, effort to explain how one can be despoiled of: nothing. This toning down of the proverb's mysterious radicality appears at a more advanced stage in Luke 8:18: "and from him who has not, *even what he thinks that he has* will be taken away." It is also modified in Gos. Thom. 88:16–18: "and whoever does not have, from him shall be taken *even the little which* he has." Both these versions attempt to explain how the nothing does not really mean nothing. But Jesus' original proverb, set in sharp and accurate parallelism, was no more and no less than an abstract statement of Basho's Staff. There is no attempt here to blur the im-mense differences between Jesus and Zen. But it must be emphasized that Jesus' use of proverbs and parables is far closer to that of Zen Buddhism than it is to conventional Hebrew wisdom.

The challenge of the historical Jesus puts language itself under strain because only paradoxical language is adequate to a message of perma-nent eschatology. Ludwig Wittgenstein, for whom aphorism was the language of philosophy, said: "There is, indeed, the inexpressible. This *shows* itself; it is the mystical." If one asks, however, how the inexpressi-ble shows itself in language itself, one has only this comment of his from another context: "Man has the urge to thrust against the limits of language. Think for instance of one's astonishment that anything exists. This astonishment cannot be expressed in the form of a question and there is no answer to it. Anything we can say must, a priori, be only nonsense. Nevertheless we thrust against the limits of language . . . But the tendency, the thrust, *points to something. . . .*"

The advent of the Kingdom not only challenges world but also under-mines language and can only be articulated in such tortured linguisticality. And this feature of Jesus' language will reappear later restated as that of the Christ: the proclaimer of God in paradox will be proclaimed as the Paradox of God. In a recent review of the modern discussion concerning the theme of apostolic incomprehension in Mark's gospel, D. J. Hawkin concluded: "Mark's task as a writer is to introduce his readership to a new scheme of things, in which ordinary values are reversed and reasonable judgments disqualified."

four

PARABLES
OF ACTION

How can his knowledge protect his desire for truth from illusion?
   How can he wait without idols to worship, without
Their overwhelming persuasion that somewhere, over the high hill,
   Under the roots of the oak, in the depths of the sea,
Is a womb or a tomb wherein he may halt to express some attainment?
   How can he hope and not dream that his solitude
Shall disclose a vibrating flame at last and entrust him forever
   With its magic secret of how to extemporize life?
                                    W. H. Auden, "For the Time Being"

In discussing the parable of the Great Supper in the last chapter, the tradition's two main tendencies toward allegorization and moralization were quite evident. It would seem that allegorization has received a much worse reception in recent scholarship than has moralization. Northrop Frye has suggested why commentators dislike allegory so much: "The commenting critic is often prejudiced against allegory without knowing the real reason, which is that continuous allegory prescribes the direction of his commentary and so restricts his freedom." In the classic work by J. Jeremias on the parables much less space and a far kinder judgment is accorded to the tradition's moralizing than to its allegorizing. On moralizing: "by the hortatory application the parable is not misinterpreted but 'actualized.'" But on allegorizing: "Jülicher . . . rid the parables of the thick layer of dust with which the allegorical interpretation had covered them." So also in more recent studies on the parables the interpretation usually avoids allegory very carefully but is still very heavy with moral application and ethical implication even if of a more existential than classical bent. All of which raises a very serious problem.

1. *Parables and Ethics*

It is hardly news that there was a very profound clash between Jesus and the Pharisees and that Paul's conversion instigated a dialectic no less violent. But later Christian animosity has badly distorted the true nature of this confrontation. Pharisees are described as hypocrites or as uncaring legalists and inhuman externalists who imposed on others burdens they themselves would not bear. Most of which is inaccurate, unhistorical, and purely polemical. If Pharisees were such, how is one to explain their tremendous power over people for whom they had only the authority of competence? In fact, the Pharisees were superb moral guides. But there precisely lay the problem which Jesus and Paul saw so clearly.

Apart from the damage such caricatures have done to Judaism and the relationship of Christianity to it, there is another very serious result within Christianity itself. When Christianity is no longer aware of what Jesus and Paul were fighting against in Pharisaic Judaism, it can hardly be conscious of a similar presence within itself. The debate did not concern good law as over against bad law or even internal and sincere law as over against external and hypocritical law. The challenge of Jesus and of Paul was this: obedience does not lead to God, but God leads one to obedience. The question is not God *or* law, covenant *or* commandment, faith *or* works, but, granting both, in which direction does the arrow fly from one to the other? It must be emphasized that this is not a debate between Judaism and Christianity but a conflict *within them both*, and a conflict ever ancient and ever new. So, according to Jesus and Paul, it was the gift of God's presence that made a good life possible, not a good life that made the reward of God's presence inevitable.

Paul's way, as everyone knows, was to proclaim human righteousness as God's free gift and that one is justified by receiving it in faith. Jesus' way was to announce the Kingdom's advent as demanding decision and response, life and action, *but* never articulating such action in detail within the parables themselves. His own life is, of course, one such actualization. For example, his association with socio-religious outcasts is a clear actualization in life of the advent-reversal-action structure of the Kingdom's presence. What Jesus proclaimed as Kingdom and Paul announced as righteousness agree, for, as Ernst Käsemann has said so succinctly: "in justification it is simply the kingdom of God proclaimed by Jesus which is at stake. His right to us is our salvation, if he does not let it drop. It will be our misfortune if we resist him. Paul's doctrine of justification is about God's *basileia*," and again elsewhere: "The righteousness of God does not presuppose our obedience; it creates it." The problem was not so much that one might not be able to obey the law's excellence but that one might actually do so to perfection and thereby be unable to tell one's own perfection from God. What exactly were Jesus and Paul fighting? In a final quotation from Käsemann: "the community of 'good' people which turns God's promises into their own privileges and God's commandments into the instruments of self-sanctification." The enemy was neither stupidity nor hypocrisy but sincerity all too sincere and perfection all too perfect.

There is a very interesting philosophical analogy to this in the question posed by Jean Beaufret to Martin Heidegger in seeking to clarify the precise relationship between ontology and a possible ethics. His answer, contained in the *Letter on Humanism*, has been summed up by B. J. Boelen: "If by ontology is meant *fundamental thinking*, the thinking of man's abode with Being . . . and by ethics man's fundamental *ēthos* (dwelling place), man's abode with Being—then fundamental thinking is *eo ipso* original ethics. In other words, fundamental ontology and original ethics are one and the same thing, and the question of their mutual relationship is therefore meaningless." One recognizes the danger of this formulation as well as the compelling challenge of its truth. One wishes in a way to scurry back for safety into well-recognized morality and more or less socially accepted ethics. In the same text, Heidegger says: "Because it thinks Being, thought thinks the Nothing." It is presumed that we have learned or are fast learning that Nothing and nothing are not the same. Wallace Stevens spoke of the "Nothing that is not there and the nothing that is." It is this "nothing that is," this Nothing, this Nothingness, that Nietzsche warned about with such terrifying accuracy: "rather than want nothing, man even wants *nothing-*

ness." To dwell with Being and seek to find in that dwelling one's morality as gift is a very, very frightening challenge. One cannot dwell with Being without dwelling also in the vicinity of Nothingness. It may be the only way, but let us be clear that it is not a very comforting one. And it is not at all clear that Jesus intended to offer any greater comfort.

The parables of Jesus seek to draw one into the Kingdom, and they challenge us to act and to live from the gift which is experienced therein. But we do not want parables. We want precepts and we want programs. We want *good* precepts and we want *sensible* programs. We are frightened by the lonely silences within the parables. Maybe if we entered into them it would be only to find, like Pompey in the Holy of Holies, that they are completely empty. We want them to tell us exactly what to do and they refuse to answer. They make us face the problem of the grounding of ethics and we want only to discuss the logic of ethics. There are very many ways in which an aphorism starting with "if any one strikes you on the right cheek" might have been finished: kill him, strike him, ignore him, forgive him, even love him. But when it is ended with "turn to him the other also" in Matt. 5:39, one is no longer giving helpful moral admonition or even radical pacifistic advice. One is deliberately overthrowing ethics in the sense in which Heidegger spoke of the necessity of overthrowing metaphysics. This aphorism brings ethics also under the radical challenge of the Kingdom. In intends us to experience how the logic of ethics is undermined by the mystery of God and that, if one can but accept it, is the most crucial moral experience of all.

The Kingdom's advent is that which undermines world so that we can experience God as distinct from world, and the action and life which the Kingdom demands is built upon this insecurity. Our ethical principles and our moral systems are absolutely necessary and so also is their inevitable shattering as part and parcel of the shattering of world. We walk a knife-edge between absolutism on the one hand and indifference on the other. All of which is rather frightening and makes one wish for just one little absolute, even one pale, frail, anaemic one to hang onto for security. But the only absolute we keep glimpsing is the Kingdom snapping our absolutes like dried twigs. So if we wish to conclude that Jesus and Paul were right against the Pharisees let us be clear about what the victory entails. Can we generate our ethics from an encounter with God knowing that any such generation is part of world and subject to ultimate judgment by the Kingdom? Can we walk and act in utter serenity and in utter insecurity, in total concern and in total incertitude?

2. *The Action Parables*

In the paradigmatic parable of the Treasure the finder discards his entire past in order to secure the field and its hidden content. Jesus' parable ends at this point: "and buys that field." There is no attempt made in Matt. 13:44 to tell us what the finder does with his newly discovered wealth. Once again, another version of the Treasure parable is very illuminating in its divergence from this. Gos. Thom. 98:31—99:3 reads: "Jesus said: The Kingdom is like a man who had a treasure [hidden] in his field, without knowing it. And [after] he died, he left it to his [son. The] son did not know (about it), he accepted that field, he sold [it]. And he who bought it, he went, while he was ploughing [he found] the treasure. He began to lend money to whomever he wished." Two points must be noted. First, as with the rabbinical story of the Treasure cited at the start of the last chapter, there is no mention of the finder selling all he had to buy the field. This would not be an item congenial to the moralizing mind in any case. The treasure was only found *after* he had bought the field and was found deservedly because it was the work of plowing which uncovered it. Second, and more to the present point, this narrative tells us what happened after the treasure's discovery: "He began to lend money to whomever he wished." It is not clear what this final phrase means in the context of the Gospel of Thomas. In itself the parable seems to show that it takes hard work to find the treasure of one's true, Gnostic self. Neither of the previous owners found it because they failed to plow the field. But the ending is a little disconcerting, especially in the light of Gos. Thom. 96:35—97:2: "If you have money, do not lend at interest, but give [them] to him from whom you will not receive them (back)." This would seem to turn the parable into a negative example against usury. In any case, and whatever the interpretation of the final admonition, it differs from Jesus' parable in detailing what the finder did with the treasure. But, as indicated at the start of this chapter, Jesus' parables challenge one to life and action within the Kingdom but they leave that life and that action as absolute in its call as it is unspecified in its detail.

This introduces the group of parables here termed "parables of action." By far the greatest number of extant parables fall into this category. This number may indicate more the interest of the primitive church than the emphasis of the historical Jesus. These were probably the type of parable most congenial to its own preaching purpose. These parables portray crucial or critical situations which demand firm and resolute action, prompt and energetic decision. The *a*morality of these parables is clear from the fact that one of them concerns a barren fig tree which finds itself in serious circumstances. In Luke 13:6–9 the tree is being given one last chance to produce fruit else it will be cut down. The difficulty of turning such parables into moral examples appears clearly in the parable of the Way to Judgment. As this is told in Luke 12:58–59 one must resolutely decide to make peace with one's judicial opponent before it is too late and one is cast into prison. As such it is an image of the resolution demanded by the Kingdom's advent. Matt. 5:25–26 turns this into a rather unhappy moral example. Keep fraternal peace lest you end up in prison. This is hardly sublime ethics in the context of Matt. 5:44 with its admonition: "Love your enemies and pray for those who persecute you, so that you may be sons of your Father who is in heaven."

Parables of action sometimes depict a situation where the decision is made, others where it is not made, and still others where some of the protagonists succeed and some fail under the pressure of the crisis. Examples of the first case, where the protagonist faces the problem and acts adequately to the situation, outnumber examples in the other two categories. But once again it is impossible to decide whether this emphasis reflects that of Jesus or of the primitive church.

Parables in which the situation meets with adequate decisional response would be the Friend at Midnight in Luke 11:5–8 and the Unjust Judge in Luke 18:2–5. In both cases one finally accepts the bothersome inevitability of what must be done. The reaper may not understand the mystery of growth, but he knows when the moment has come and he must hasten to harvest. This is usually referred to as the Seed Growing Secretly in Mark 4:26–29. Most likely, however, the general context created by the preceding seed parable of the Sower in Mark 4:3–8 and the following one of the Mustard Seed in 4:30–32 has placed an emphasis on the seed in 4:26–29 which was not there originally. The earlier version would have kept the emphasis strictly on the farmer as in 4:26,

27, 29, before the addition of 4:28. In the version of this parable in Gos. Thom. 85:15–19: "Let there be among you a man of understanding; when the fruit ripened, he came quickly with his sickle in his hand, he reaped it. Whoever has ears to hear let him hear," the emphasis is totally on the farmer. The better title might be the parable of the Reaper. So also the homeowner who has prior warning of the coming of the Thief will know exactly what to do and will act accordingly, in Matt. 24:43–44 and Luke 12:39–40. This parable is also in Gos. Thom. 85:7–10 and 98:6–10. In the former situation it immediately precedes the parable of the Reaper. Even in the very delicate problem of the Wheat and the Darnel in Matt. 13:24–30, the wise farmer knows better than to follow the suggestion of his well-meaning servants and let them attempt to root out the darnel from among the young wheat. He lets them both grow until the harvest and then he has both his wheat safe and some free kindling as well. His enemy is doubly outwitted. Similar prudent reactions appear in the Tower Builder and the Campaign Planner parables in Luke 14:28–32.

There are other parables in which the person involved fails completely to realize the situation and the call to action stands forth in rather negative coloring. Such is the case of the Rich Fool in Luke 12:16–20 and Gos. Thom. 92:3–10. Luke's general context makes this a negative example where one has chosen material goods over against God. This is emphasized by the succeeding comment in 12:21: "So is he who lays up treasure for himself, and is not rich toward God." It also shows up in the tonality of the man's address to his "Soul" in 12:19 and God's calling him "Fool" in 12:20. But that in Gos. Thom. 92:3–10 is a simple story of tragic irony in which a man spends his last day on earth planning a long future. A very definite but utterly human example of failure to realize one's true situation. It is the same with the man who lacks a Wedding Garment in Matt. 22:11–14, which was originally a quite separate parable of action. What do you think would happen to such a man? The result is disastrous in all these cases.

There is also the possibility of a parable which shows forcibly both responses within the same situation. For example, in that of the Bridesmaids in Matt. 25:1–13, five are wise to the possible problems of their function and prepare accordingly while five others fail to take adequate precautions and miss the wedding banquet.

Apart from these parables of action just noted there is one whole set which might be called Servant parables. These involve a master-servant relationship at a moment of critical reckoning. The rest of this chapter will be a detailed study of this set of parables. The first step will be a complete analysis of the parable of the Wicked Husbandmen. This parable will then be situated within the broader context of the Servant parables, all of which are parables of action.

3. The Wicked Husbandmen

This parable deserves very special attention. As the Good Samaritan had seemed to be the purest instance of a moral example or exemplary story from Jesus, so this parable is, apparently, the most perfect example of allegory from his historical teaching. Even authors who think that Jesus did not normally use allegory conclude that this is the one striking exception. Unlike the Sower, for example, where the allegorical interpretation is even textually separated from the parable and where one would hardly be expected to know without its help that "the birds" of Mark 4:4 are actually "Satan" as explained in 4:15, this parable has the allegory built into the very text itself—or so it would seem. Other authors who insist that this is not an allegory but a parable have had little success in explaining it as such and, in effect, have usually interpreted it allegorically while hailing it as a parable. More will be seen on this at the end of the analysis.

The parable is found in both the synoptic tradition of Mark 12:1–12, which is the common source for Matt. 21:33–46 and Luke 20:9–19, and also in Gos. Thom. 93:1–18, in an independent version. Since this parable is of such theoretical importance, the full text will be given for both these versions as the study proceeds.

(1) The Synoptic Tradition. The purpose of this section is to draw attention to conceptual strains within the synoptic tradition when this story is read as an allegory. The question is not whether every single element can be shown to have individual allegorical significance but whether any of the larger points seem to distract from or even strain against the main thrust of the allegory itself. The story has seven main elements and these will be investigated in succession.

(a) Construction of the Vineyard. Mark 12:1 reads: " 'A man planted a vineyard, and set a hedge around it, and dug a pit for the wine press, and built a tower, and let it out to tenants, and went into another country.' " The vineyard's construction is evidently based on that in the song of Isa. 5:2 from the Greek translation of the Hebrew Bible. Here the prophet allegorizes Israel as the vineyard of God which has yielded only wild grapes. Matt. 21:33 follows Mark 12:1 in mentioning the planting and the fencing, the digging of the winepress, and the building of the watchtower. All four points derive explicitly from the Greek text of Isa. 5:2. This derivation is much less clear in Luke 20:9 and remains only residually visible in his "planted a vineyard." In the second part of the verse all three gospels agree: "and let it out to tenants, and went into another country." Luke 20:9b adds "for a long while." This is his own addition since the Greek word used for "long" is almost exclusively his in the New Testament. The addition could be a reference to the long time which must elapse before the return of Jesus at the end of the world. This would certainly confuse the allegory even more since the absent owner is supposed to be God. It seems better to consider the addition as a simple attempt to add some "realism" to the story.

(b) Mission of the Servants. The text in Mark 12:2–5 reads: " 'When the time came, he sent a servant to the tenants, to get from them some of the fruit of the vineyard. And they took him and beat him, and sent him away empty-handed. Again he sent to them another servant, and they wounded him in the head, and treated him shamefully. And he sent another, and him they killed; and so with many others, some they beat and some they killed.' " The mission of the servants is told more soberly in Luke 20:10–12. Here there are only three successive servants, "a servant . . . another servant . . . a third." Nobody is killed, but the three are, respectively, beaten, beaten and treated shamefully, wounded and cast out, so that there is a certain climactic gravity to the damage done as the story proceeds. But at least one does not have the problem in the Markan account: why keep sending individual servants after some are killed? Neither Matthew nor Luke follow Mark's strange detail concerning the wounding in the head. It seems a rather deliberate redactional insertion by Mark himself to allude to the fate of the beheaded Baptist in Mark 6:27. The death of the Baptist was extremely important for Mark's theology as it set the divinely established pattern for the fate of Jesus himself and of those who would follow him. The detail represents Mark's contribution to the allegory of salvation history he has received from the tradition. His original text probably had three statements: a servant who was *beaten;* a servant who was *killed;* and many others some of whom were *beaten* and some *killed.* But apparently in all this we are dealing with single servants sent successively. This is drastically changed in Matt. 21:34–36. There are no single servants but two clearly distinguished groups of servants, "his servants . . . other servants, more than the first." The first group is beaten, killed, and stoned, and so is the second set. Matthew's addition to Mark's catalogue of evil is the stoning.

At this point it is clear that the servant-messengers are being moved in different directions in the synoptic transmission. Mark is not interested in sharpening the allegorical servants as Old Testament prophets but in adding the Baptist to the list of the rejected ones. Matthew is developing a precise allegorical application in which the first group of servants is the early prophets and the second group is the later ones. Hence both groups are treated alike. Luke's literary sensitivities react strongly to all this and his version is much more realistic: three single servants come and nobody is killed. But it is already obvious that story and allegory do not fit too well. Single servants are becoming groups of servants and rejections are being changed into murders.

(c) The Mission of the Son. Mark 12:6–7 reads: " 'He had still one other, a beloved son; finally he sent him to them, saying, "They will respect my son." But those tenants said to one another, "This is the heir; come, let us kill him, and the inheritance will be ours." ' " Following through the allegory of salvation history, the son who is sent last of all is Jesus. Mark, followed by Luke 20:13–14 but not Matt. 21:37–38, stresses this identity by the term "beloved" which recalls this term as used of Jesus by God at the Baptism in Mark 1:11 and during the Transfiguration in 9:7. But three points stand out with some strangeness against this allegorical background. What is the function of the words "respect," "heir," and "inheritance"? These words are found in the three synoptic accounts and yet they hardly seem normal in the allegorical setting. Did God the Father expect only "respect" for Jesus? And was Jesus actually killed by those who wished thereby to obtain some divine inheritance? The allegory is now straining very badly at the seams. The argument is not that every single element in the allegory has to be significant and meaningful. It is surely possible that some points render service to others which are themselves of direct allegorical purpose. But,

knowing beforehand the history or dogma one wishes to portray allegorically, one should not create elements on the literal level which positively
clash with meanings on the allegorical level. The son sent last of all is
a perfect allegorical representation of Jesus and the idea of Jesus as the
heir of God is not problematic. One recalls the words of Heb. 1:2: "in
these *last* days he has spoken to us by a Son, whom he appointed the
heir of all things." The real difficulty is the weakness of the motivation
theme. What is the meaning of "respect" for the Father, and what are
the hopes of "inheritance" for the tenants?

(d) The Death of the Son. Mark 12:8 reads: " 'And they took him
and killed him, and cast him out of the vineyard.' " It has just been
noted that the Synoptic Gospels agree on the motivation of the son's
murder. The only important change in the details of his death is again
due to an intensification of the allegory. Mark had the tenants murder
him and throw the unburied body outside the vineyard. This means no
more than an underlining of their evil action. But Matt. 21:39 and Luke
20:15a, independently changing Mark, bring the story closer to allegorical actuality by having the son taken outside the vineyard and there
killed, just as Jesus was taken and crucified outside the walls of Jerusalem.

(e) Punishment of the Tenants. Mark 12:9 reads: " 'What will the
owner of the vineyard do? He will come and destroy the tenants, and
give the vineyard to others.' " The punishment of the tenants is told in
a question-and-answer format. Matt. 21:40–41 and Luke 20:15b–16
agree with Mark in calling the owner here *kyrios*, although they had
called him simply "a man" or "a householder" at the start of the parable.
They also agree in posing the question with "what will [he] do?" Mark
and Luke agree on a two-point answer and it is given by Jesus himself.
Matthew has a three-point answer and it is given by the hearers themselves in answer to Jesus' question: "He will put those wretches to a
miserable death, and let out the vineyard to other tenants who will give
him the fruits in their seasons."

Once again the allegory seems under considerable strain. The changes
in Matthew can easily be explained as an allusion to the divided state
of his own church and the mention of the necessary fruits is a warning
against complacency. This same purpose had made him add the parable
of the Wedding Garment in 22:11–14 to that of the Great Supper in
22:1–10. But even the two-point answer in Mark and Luke is prob-

lematic. Is it likely that the owner after such an experience would give his vineyard out again to any tenants? This item is dictated by the actualities of the Gentile mission rather than by the possibilities and probabilities of agrarian experience. The vineyard is taken from Israel and given to the Gentiles. Indeed, the whole idea of this punitive expedition by the master is very improbable against the rest of the story. If such power had always been available to him, the pathetic hope for respect becomes somewhat ludicrous. The punishment theme is an allegorization of the influx of Gentiles into the church. Finally, this theme has been formulated with two points which recall the vineyard allegory from Isaiah. As Mark 12:1, at the start, refers to Isa. 5:2, so now Mark 12:9, at the end, alludes to Isa. 5:4, 5, 7. The "owner [*kyrios*] of the vineyard" in 12:9 links with the "vineyard of the Lord [*Kyrios*]" of Isa. 5:7. And the "what will [he] do?" of 12:9 points to the repeated question, "what . . . to do," and "what I will do," of Isa. 5:4, 5. Hence the synoptic allegory is closed in these verses with allusions to the original prophetic allegory.

Once again the major problem is that, while the allegory suits well the historical actualities of primitive church experience, it is rather disharmonious with the "logic" of the story itself. Whence this sudden change from impotence to vengeance on the part of the owner, and why rent out the vineyard again after such an experience?

(f) Citation from Ps. 118:22–23. The text in Mark 12:10–11 is a Psalm citation: " 'Have you not read this scripture: "The very stone which the builders rejected has become the head of the corner; this was the Lord's doing, and it is marvelous in our eyes"?' " Matt. 21:42–43 follows Mark but Luke 20:17–18 copies only Ps. 118:22 and then changes the ending. The citation from Ps. 118 was an obvious necessity of the allegorical situation. The end could not be the death of the son, even when his murder had been amply punished. The end would have to be the triumph of the son. The apologetic of the stone rejected by the builders but made the cornerstone by act of God is well known from the preaching of the early church. This quotation is now added to effect this victorious conclusion. But it is also quite clear that the triumph of the son does not really appear *within* the allegory itself but is added to it in this proof-text. It would seem unlikely that any allegorization of the story was possible until, first and above all, the death of the son had been changed into triumph. This mention of victory for the son is even more important than any note concerning punishment or replacement.

(g) Application to the Authorities. As the story ends in Mark 12:12, Matt. 21:45–46, and Luke 20:19 the allegorical and the historical cross each other openly. Mark reads: "And they tried to arrest him, but feared the multitude, for they perceived that he had told the parable against them; so they left him and went away." The authorities recognize that the parable is an allegory directed against them as the wicked tenants.

The unit is clearly an allegory in the synoptic tradition. God's vineyard will be taken from the evil authorities of Israel and given to the Gentiles. These authorities have rejected the prophets of old and killed Jesus whom God has now made the cornerstone. The allegory of Mark is intensified in Matthew but muted into greater "realism" by Luke. Two very important questions are left to be answered. First, if the allegory stemmed from Jesus as a prophecy of his own impending death, what was his purpose in mentioning the motivation of the father's sending of the son (respect) and of the tenants' murder of the son (inheritance)? Second, if the allegory came only from the creativity of the primitive church, the above question still holds and an even more serious difficulty is added. Could such an allegory have been constructed in the early church without some allusion to Jesus' resurrectional victory being built *intrinsically* into the story itself and not just added to it externally by the stone-text? For example, one might imagine a vague mention of the son's being rejected, like John 1:11, "received him not," so that afterward he might return in the power of his father and take back the vineyard. Even allowing for creative work with one eye on the allegory of Isa. 5:1–7 and the other on salvation history up to the present of the writer, there are problematic discrepancies in the narrative, and the point that sticks above all is the meaning of the theme of inheritance.

(2) The Gospel of Thomas. The preceding problems might not be sufficient to cast doubt on the originality of the allegorical interpretation of the story or to support the present contention that it is an attempt to turn parable into allegory that has caused them. One might easily object that similar inconsistencies are to be found in rabbinical parables. At most they might indicate the creator's literary incompetence. But the presence of a version of this story in Gos. Thom. 93:1–18 becomes

extremely important at this point, precisely because no such discrepancies or inconsistencies can be found in its construction. This is the full text:

He said: A good man had a vineyard. He gave it to husbandmen so that they would work it and that he would receive its fruit from them. He sent his servant so that the husbandmen would give him the fruit of the vineyard. They seized his servant, they beat him; a little longer and they would have killed him. The servant came, he told it to his master. His master said: "Perhaps he did not know them" [or: "Perhaps they did not recognize him"]. He sent another servant; the husbandmen beat him as well. Then the owner sent his son. He said: "Perhaps they will respect my son." Since those husbandmen knew that he was the heir of the vineyard, they seized him, they killed him. Whoever has ears let him hear. Jesus said: Show me the stone which the builders have rejected; it is the corner-stone.

In turning from the "strained" allegory in the synoptic tradition to this story here certain features are immediately evident. First, there are no allusions to Isa. 5:1–7 at the start or conclusion of the story. Second, only single servants are sent, only two are sent, and nobody is killed before the murder of the son, even though there is a literary warning of this event with the first servant: "a little longer and they would have killed him." Third, there is no mention of the son being killed or thrown "outside the vineyard." Fourth, there is no concluding question and answer and, therefore, no mention of the punishment of the tenants. After the murder there is only the concluding phrase "Whoever has ears let him hear." From all this it is clear that there is no overt allegory *within* the story in this version. On the other hand, it contains both the theme of respect and of inheritance as in the synoptic tradition, and in almost the same language: "He said: 'Perhaps they will respect my son.' Since those husbandmen knew that he was the heir of the vineyard, they seized him, they killed him." As the story stands here, there is no reason to look on it as an allegory at all.

(a) Gos. Thom. 93:1–16 and 17–18. An immediate problem is 93:1–16 as followed by 93:17–18. Just as the stone-text from Ps. 118 was appended in the synoptic tradition in order to complete the allegory, so too this version has in 93:17–18: "Jesus said: Show me the stone which the builders have rejected; it is the corner-stone." It might be argued that this also reflects on the preceding unit and thereby allegorizes it at least from without. But one must note the presence of 93:16, "Whoever has ears let him hear." This is used to terminate the story which was introduced by the "Jesus said" of 93:1, and, after it, a new saying is introduced with another "Jesus said" in 93:17–18. This is exactly the same usage of the saying "Whoever has ears let him hear" as elsewhere in Gos. Thom. 82:2; 85:19; 92:9; and 97:6, where it concludes a parable and precedes a new and independent saying with "Jesus said." The only other usage of the saying is in 86:6 and there it introduces a parabolic saying. From all of this it would seem that the parable in 93:1–16 is clearly distinguished by the author from the new and disconnected stone-text in 93:17–18. This does not necessarily deny that both units may refer to true gnosis: to the persecution of the gnostic in 93:1–16 and to the triumph of the gnostic in 93:17–18.

But it is rather too much to presume that the quotation from Ps. 118 just happened to be in exactly the same place in both Mark and the Gospel of Thomas. It is much more likely that the earliest stage of the allegorization process involved this *external* juxtaposition of an allusion to the triumph of Jesus to the murder story. Further allegorization *within* the story could hardly have proceeded until the basic story no longer ended with the son's murder but with the son's victory. In other words, the conjunction of 93:1–16 and 17–18 as the earliest stage of the allegorization process was already available to the Gospel of Thomas or its source. But, whether he understood it or not, he did not accept it, and instead he made two completely separate units out of it. The artificial joining of the units with its mixing of metaphors (Jesus as son, Jesus as stone) would have rendered this separation all the easier. Hence, the story of 93:1–16 must be studied as a unit complete in itself.

(b) The Structure of Gos. Thom. 93:1–15. This narrative has four movements: the setting, the first servant, the second servant, the son. The setting could hardly be more terse. The second servant is needed to make the folkloric threesome and so adds nothing of detail to the story. The son's mission is very close to the version in the synoptic tradition.

All of this focuses attention on the first servant and here things are strikingly different from the synoptic tradition. The statement: "The servant came, he told it to his master. His master said: 'Perhaps they did not recognize him,' " (using the alternative reading) has no parallel at all in the synoptic tradition and is the only unit which does not have a parallel there. Second, the incident of the first servant is longer than that of the other three units in the structure and quantitative stress is given to this even over the mission of the son himself. Third, there are formal similarities between the narrative concerning the first servant and that of the son. There is in each case, a sending, a result, and a comment by the master. The formal similarity appears not only in the triple structure of the elements but even more precisely in the comparative content of the three elements. "He sent his servant" leads to "sent his son." The clause "a little longer and they would have killed him" prepares for the final statement "they killed him." The phrase "His master said: 'Perhaps they did not recognize him' " explains the later statement "He said: 'Perhaps they will respect my son.' " All of this structural analysis serves to raise a question of some importance. Why so much space given and given so carefully to the first servant?

It is a cliché in parable analysis that such stories must be true to life, either to the recurrent actualities or the recognizable possibilities of experience and existence. The problematic situation of Gos. Thom. 93:1–15 is perfectly reasonable and, as we now know, even quite possible against the historical actualities of Galilee's absentee landlords and rebellious peasantry at the time of Jesus. But it might still seem totally improbable that the owner would send his son into such a dangerous situation without some protection greater than that given to the servants. It is here that the master's reaction to the first servant becomes vitally important, and indeed indispensable, to the story's credibility. The master presumes that the problem is that the tenants will not acknowledge ("recognize"), be it in good faith or bad, the authority of the servant to collect for their master. This may even be the reason why he is called a "good man" at the start of the parable. He does not at all presume evil let alone lethal intent. Hence it is eventually necessary to send the son with the hope that they will accept his authority and respect his mission. From a literary point of view the excessive space given the first servant is quite justifiable. It establishes credibility for the succeeding events and it prepares, in both form and content, for the final climactic murder of the son.

(c) Gos. Thom. 93:1–15 and the Synoptics. At this point it would seem clear that this story is quite independent from the version found in the synoptic tradition. If one held that Gos. Thom. 93:1–15 is dependent on the synoptics, one might argue that the author removed all their allegorical features to turn it into a parable warning the true gnostic against persecution for himself or as an example against material lust in others. This might be persuasive if that was all he had done. Even if one were ready to accept as coincidence the fact that he pared the story back to the folkloric threesome, there is still the problem of the section concerning the first servant. This addition is unexplained on the hypothesis of synoptic dependence. The best solution is that Gos. Thom. 93:1–15 is giving a very early and quite independent version of a parable of Jesus. This parable was gradually allegorized before and during the synoptic tradition and this process resulted in a growing strain between the logic of the original story and the necessities of the allegory.

(3) The Original Meaning. A glance at some recent analyses of the parable might be useful at this point. It is of great importance, of course, whether the original story is taken to have included the Isaiah allusions or not, and it is of equal importance to decide where did the original version end: with the crime or with the punishment. C. H. Dodd includes both the Isaiah references and the question, but not the answer, in the authentic parable of Jesus. He then interprets it as a warning concerning his own coming death. At which stage one has to agree with the wry comment of M. Black: "while thus showing allegory firmly to the door, one cannot but wonder if Dr. Dodd has not surreptitiously smuggled it in by the window." J. Jeremias considers both the Isaiah allusions and the question/answer which introduces the punishment theme and the replacement theme as being secondary. But in a rather flagrant contradiction he uses the former implicitly and the latter explicitly to explain the parable as Jesus' vindication of the gospel offered to the poor as the vineyard is taken away from the evil authorities of Israel. This problem was already noted by J. J. Vincent in his comment: "Does Jeremias in fact avoid the allegorization which he seeks to root out? If 'the others' are 'the poor' and the tenants are the leaders of the people, why should not the servants be the prophets and the son Jesus?" D. O. Via takes a position between these two authors by eliminating the detailed reference to Isaiah while retaining the punishment theme. Hence he understands it as referring to the Jerusalem authorities and,

once again, it is an allegory of the historical Jesus. But, *methodologically,* J. Jeremias was surely correct in eliminating both Isaiah and punishment, as in Gos. Thom. 93:1–15, from the original version. Why then did they slip back into the interpretation? The answer would seem to be that otherwise Jesus is telling a most disedifying and immoral story, even if it is quite possible or even historically actual within the Galilean experience of his time. But it is more likely that he was doing this than that he was rather awkwardly allegorizing his own death.

When, however, it is decided that Gos. Thom. 93:1–15 is the best version of the original parable which we have extant at the moment, its meaning is quite clear as a parable of action. It is a deliberately shocking story of successful murder. The story is certainly possible and possibly actual in the Galilean turbulence of the period. It tells of some people who recognized their situation, saw their opportunity, and acted resolutely upon it. They glimpsed a way of getting full possession of the vineyard by murdering the only heir and, with murderous speed, they moved to accomplish their purpose.

4. *The Servant Parables*

The parable of the Wicked Husbandmen will now be integrated into the wider background of what will be called the Servant parables of Jesus. These are all parables of action but they also demonstrate very strikingly the relationship of these parables to the preceding parables of reversal.

(1) The Theme of the Servant. The thematic unity of the Servant parables revolves around two poles. They all concern a master-servant relationship *and* a time or moment of critical reckoning therein. It makes no difference whether the servant is a minor household slave or a major state official as long as there is a real superior-subordinate crisis involved. No special term is required for the servant, therefore, and even if Jesus had consistently used a given word in such parables, the tradition might not have consistently preserved it. For example, in the parable of the Overseer from the source Q, Matt. 24:45–51 always calls him a "servant," but Luke 12:42–46 begins by calling him a "steward" and then slips back into the source's word "servant" for the rest of the story.

The Servant parables do not include, on the other hand, those parables where servants are present but where the story does not revolve around a critical reckoning between master and servant. For example, one would not include the Great Supper here even though there are servant-messengers mentioned in Matt. 22:1–10 and Luke 14:16–24, or the Wedding Garment despite the "attendants" of Matt. 22:13. Neither would one include other parables where servants play only minor roles and there is no critical confrontation between them and their master. Thereby excluded would be such parables as the Wheat and the Darnel in Matt. 13:24–30, the Prodigal Son in Luke 15:11–32, or the Way to Judgment in Matt. 5:25–26 or Luke 12:58–59, despite the presence of servants or minor officials within the story. Only parables containing both points as their central story-line are to be included in the theme: a superior-subordinate relationship *and* a crisis of reckoning within this relationship.

Nine parables will be studied within this thematic unity. The order in which they will be presented is intended to show as clearly as possible the point to be made. It is not implied that Jesus created them in this sequence or even uttered them in this specific order. No matter in what order they are taken their thematic unity reflects backward and forward from one to the other. Together they form a musical harmony, as it were, in which no single one is heard adequately until all are heard fully. This comparative and cumulative reading on a musical analogy is like the reading of the thematically united myths in the work of C. Lévi-Strauss. Indeed, this type of reading on the analogy of an orchestral score appears in many other areas of language. So Jacques Lacan, as cited before: "But one has only to listen to poetry . . . to know in fact that all discourse aligns itself along the several staves of a score." Even more to the general thesis of this section is his later comment within the same writing: "One thing this structure of the signifying chain makes evident is the possibility I have, precisely insofar as I have this language in common with other subjects, that is insofar as it exists as a language, to use it in order to say something quite other than what it says. This function of the word is more worth pointing out than that of 'disguising the thought' (more often than not indefinable) of the subject; it is no less than the function of indicating the place of the subject in the search for the truth." What we shall be watching in this section is Jesus slowly developing a parabolic *theme*, not just a proverb or a single parable, into its own polar reversal. The theme will end up saying "something quite other than what it says" and this will indicate very clearly for us "the place of the subject [Jesus] in the search for the truth."

(2) The Development of the Theme. The first cluster of parables, called Group A for easy reference, consists of the Doorkeeper, the Overseer, the Talents, and the Throne Claimant. As with all the parables studied in this book, the first effort must be directed to establishing the general content, but not of course the exact words, of the original parable as spoken by the historical Jesus.

(a) The Doorkeeper. This parable is contained in a rather changed format in two independent versions. One helps to end Mark's eschatological discourse in Mark 13:33–37:

Take heed, watch; for you do not know when the time will come. It is like a man going on a journey, when he leaves home and puts his servants in charge, each with his work, and commands the doorkeeper to be on the watch. Watch therefore—for you do not know when the master of the house will come, in the evening, or at midnight, or at cockcrow, or in the morning—lest he come suddenly and find you asleep. And what I say to you I say to all: Watch.

The other version is now part of Luke's teaching of the disciples in Luke 12:35–38:

Let your loins be girded and your lamps burning, and be like men who are waiting for their master to come home from the marriage feast, so that they may open to him at once when he comes and knocks. Blessed are those servants whom the master finds awake when he comes; truly, I say to you, he will gird himself and have them sit at table, and he will come and serve them. If he comes in the second watch, or in the third, and finds them so, blessed are those servants.

Despite their independent development in the tradition and despite their final redactional modifications the narrative lineaments of a coherent story can be discerned behind both versions. Indeed, it takes both to make one good story. Both accounts now appear as third-person narratives embedded in second-person injunctions. This is evident in even a cursory reading of the above texts. In both cases the return of the master is associated with the coming of the Son of Man, earlier in

Mark 13:26 and later in Luke 12:40. But in both cases the present versions and situations of the story contain some rather unlikely elements and these jar the "realism" demanded of parables. First, in Mark: A doorkeeper is expected to keep watch night and day for a departed master who may return at any time. Then, in Luke: The servants (all of them?) have only to watch for a master returning that night from a feast but when and if they do their duty they will be served at table by the grateful master. Clearly the association of returning master and coming Son of Man has changed the story so as to render some of its elements quite unlikely. We are on the way to another "strained" allegory.

The basic story, the debris of a parable of Jesus, is still quite visible behind these changes. The master departs for a nighttime feast, maybe even a wedding feast. He enjoins the servant who is the doorkeeper to watch so as to expedite his returning entrance. The later the return is, the more difficult will it be for the doorkeeper to stay awake, but also the more important will it be that he be awake. This accepts the situation of the nighttime feast of Luke rather than the vague and general "going on a journey" of Mark. It accepts the single servant, the doorkeeper, of Mark rather than the plural servants of Luke. Finally, it prefers the timing of the return in Luke (second or third watch) to the fourfold possibility given in Mark. One will hardly return from a nighttime feast in the first watch, or at sunset. The story is coherent, possible, and even mildly humorous. There is the inference that the returning master will need even more assistance, and therefore preparatory watchfulness, the later the hour at which he seeks to find the door, or the house, or maybe even the village. The implicit theme of punishment for failure ("lest . . .") in Mark 13:36 appears in Luke as reward at the eschatological banquet, but, no doubt, this theme of sanction is basic to the entire situation even if not explicitly mentioned.

(b) The Overseer. The parable is found in Matt. 24:45–51 and Luke 12:42–46, and it comes from the Q text. The two versions are very similar. This is Luke:

Who then is the faithful and wise steward, whom his master will set over his household, to give them their portion of food at the proper time? Blessed is that servant whom his master when he comes will find so doing. Truly I tell you, he will set him over all his possessions. But if that servant says to himself, "My master is delayed in coming," and begins to beat the menservants and the maidservants, and to eat and drink and get drunk, the master of that servant will come on a day when he does not expect him and at an hour he does not know, and will punish him, and put him with the unfaithful.

The parable balances a positive and negative possibility within the imagined situation of the same single servant, an overseer. The positive (good or faithful) and negative (bad or faithless) reactions of the servant are carefully integrated so that the hearer can easily imagine both possibilities. It is the temptation afforded by the master's delay in returning that might turn a good servant into a bad one. Hence, Matt. 24:48 and Luke 12:45a are crucial for the integrity and "realism" of the story. This point may fit well into the problem of the delay in the return of the Son of Man at the parousia but it did not derive from that problem. Without its presence the change of the good servant into an evil one is left unexplained and the parable starts to break into the story of two servants, one good and one bad. Much of its persuasive force is then lost.

The positive reaction in the first half of the story has three moments: the commission, the return, and the reward. So also the negative alternative in the second half of the story has three corresponding points: the omission, the return, and the punishment. It should be noted how carefully the parable stays within the realistic possibilities of such a master-servant situation.

(c) The Talents. The parable is given in Matt. 25:14–30 and Luke 19:12–27. Since the story is so long and the two versions so different, they will not be given here.

Two separate parables have been fused, and not too happily, in Luke 19:12–27. The parable of the Talents (or Minas, or whatever the original monetary unit was) appears in 19:12a, 13, 15b–26, and that of the Throne Claimant in 19:12b, 14–15a, 27. The rewarding of the servants by their appointment over various cities in 19:17, 19, represents an intrusion from the Throne Claimant theme into the subject of the Talents or Minas parable. There is no trace of the Throne Claimant parable in Matt. 25:14–30, and it is quite unlikely that he would have carefully removed it had he found it already fused in the Q text. Most likely, then, Matthew and Luke did not get this parable from Q but from their own special and independent sources. The Throne Claimant will be left aside for the moment and the two versions of the Talents (Matthew) and the Minas (Luke) compared. The parable has been called that of the Talents since it has been traditionally known by that name but the amount given in Luke is much more "realistic."

It is clear that there is a common narrative behind the separate versions of Matthew and Luke. This can be shown in two major areas. First, the structure of the story and the sequence of the elements are completely parallel. There is the situation, the return and reckoning, the first servant rewarded, the second servant rewarded, and the third servant punished. Second, there are striking similarities in the incident of the third servant, in sequence, in concepts, and most especially in vocabulary. Notice the following *common* phrases in Matt. 25:24–29 and Luke 19:20–26: "reaping where/what you did not sow; I was afraid; You wicked servant; you knew that; my money with the bankers/into the bank; and at my coming . . . with interest; take . . . from him, and give it to him who has; to every one who has will more be given . . . but from him who has not, even what he has will be taken away." The basic parable shows clearly through the variants, and even the minor differences do not destroy this general similarity.

Two differences are of more importance. First, there is the presence of Matt. 25:16–18 which has no parallel in Luke: "He who had received the five talents went at once and traded with them; and he made five talents more. So also, he who had the two talents made two talents more. But he who had received the one talent went and dug in the ground and hid his master's money." This tells what the three servants did while the master was away. Is this original or did Matthew add it himself? The content is not specifically Matthean either in concept or vocabulary and came to him most probably in his source. Indeed, the dramatic value of 25:16–18 within the unfolding of the narrative argues for its originality. It has two functions. The contrast between the first two servants and the third one is immediately established, and questions are immediately posed for the hearer's mind. Why did the third one do this (to be answered in 25:24–25) and what will happen because of it (to be answered in 25:26–28)? The result of having 25:16–18 present is to draw the hearer immediately into the world of the parable so that already one is taking sides, pondering, wondering, and questioning.

A second question concerns the original ending of the parable. One can immediately omit Luke 19:27 since it is part of the Throne Claimant parable and had originally nothing to do with the Talents story. One must also omit Matt. 25:30 as the original ending because of its allegorical character, explicit eschatological application, and Matthean vocabulary. Luke has no parallel to it. It reads: "And cast the worthless servant into the outer darkness; there men will weep and gnash their teeth." Neither is the original conclusion to be found in the common verse of Matt. 25:29 and Luke 19:25–26. It was seen elsewhere in this book that this saying concerning giving to one who has and taking from one who has not is an independent or free-floating saying of Jesus found both in Q, whence it is taken here, but also in Mark 4:25, whence it was copied into Matt. 13:12 and Luke 8:18. It really does not even fit very well with the present story on two details. First, only the first servant, but not the second one, receives any increment from the third servant's failure. Second, the third servant does in fact have something to be taken away from him. This leaves Matt. 25:28 = Luke 19:24 as the original ending of the parable. It reads: "Take the talent/mina from him, and give it to him who has the ten talents/minas." This has the compositional advantage of returning the parable to its beginning so that Matt. 25:28 recalls 25:20 ("And he who had received the five talents came forward") and also the inaugural 25:15 ("to one he gave five talents").

The main story is quite clear as is its use of the standard folkloric threesome. Two servants are rewarded for their work and a third is punished for his prudent if useless inactivity. The structural rhythm of the story is very evident in the Matthean account and we can conclude with a glance at its careful choreography:

	Scene 1	Scene 2	Scene 3
Situation	25:14	25:15d	25:19
Servant 1:	25:15a	25:16	25:20–21
Servant 2:	25:15b	25:17	25:22–23
Servant 3:	25:15c	25:18	25:24–28

In Scene 1 there is one main verb: "gave." In Scene 2 there are two main ones: "made" and "hid." In Scene 3 these last two verbs beget two others: "made" begets "set you" and "hid" begets "take from him."

(d) The Throne Claimant. As was just seen, the remains of an originally separate parable concerning a Throne Claimant was fused with the parable of the Talents/Minas in Luke. We no longer know the full text of this parable but what can be seen in Luke 19:12b, 14–15a, 27, reads as follows:

(A nobleman went into a far country) to receive kingly power and then return. But his citizens hated him and sent an embassy after him, saying, "We do not want this man to reign over us." When he returned, having received the kingly power. . . . But as for those enemies of mine, who did not want me to reign over them, bring them here and slay them before me.

The category of Servant parables will have to include this one as well. It concerns a superior-subordinate ("nobleman . . . citizens") relationship in a critical confrontation. The very fact that it was fused with the other Servant parable of the Talents/Minas points it toward this grouping.

The historical background of the parable is well known. In the words of J. Jeremias: "[it is a] parable about a claimant for the throne, reflecting the historical situation of 4 B.C. At that time Archelaus journeyed to Rome to get his kingship over Judaea confirmed; at the same time a Jewish embassy of fifty persons also went to Rome in order to resist his appointment. The sanguinary revenge inflicted upon the people by Archelaus after his return had never been forgotten." It is already obvious from the master in the parable of the Talents ("a hard man" in Matt. 25:24) that Jesus was interested in realistic rather than idealistic masters. So there should be no surprise at his use of Archelaus here. There is no presumption in this group of parables that general morality is under discussion. Such terms as "good and bad," "reward or punishment," pertain exclusively within the world of the parable and within the master-servant relationship which forms the thematic parameter of the series.

(3) The Reversal of the Development. The four parables investigated so far have a certain *normalcy* about them. Good or faithful or successful servants are rewarded; bad and faithless and unsuccessful servants are punished. Each can be presumed to have known and expected such an outcome. In the Doorkeeper parable, punishment is left implicit in Mark 13:36 and reward noted explicitly in Luke 12:38. In the original

version the sanctions may have been left totally implicit. In the next two parables there is an explicit division into good rewarded and bad punished. This is carefully balanced and evenly stressed in the Overseer and the Talents. So also with the Throne Claimant. The citizen-servants who had opposed his accession were punished for their infidelity upon his return as king. Whatever the meaning and intention of these parables, they all seem to move in a quite expected and normal manner. It makes little difference to this normalcy whether the point is that the servant should recognize his situation and act accordingly or the point is the promise and threat of reward and punishment. In either case we move within a horizon of expected orderly and orderly expectation. The servant can only know how to act on the presumptive correlation of good with reward and bad with punishment.

There is, however, a second cluster of parables, Group B, in which this horizon of expected normalcy is not so apparent and in which this development of the theme in Group A is questioned, probed, and finally contradicted. This second set includes the Unmerciful Servant, the Servant's Reward, the Unjust Steward, the Wicked Husbandmen, seen already in an earlier section, and the Vineyard Workers. The Unmerciful Servant begins with a bad servant who is *not* going to be punished because of the master's pity. But when he fails to act accordingly with his own debtor, the master reverses his original decision and punishes him quite adequately. The parable has deviated from the expected normalcy of Group A on one level and yet reverted to it again on a second level. One agrees that this is how it could (would? should?) be. This parable serves as a good transition from Group A to Group B. The Servant's Reward introduces a flat contradiction to the previous development in Group A. Even good servants are not rewarded. The Unjust Steward and the Wicked Husbandmen move even more basically away from the expected normalcy. In both cases bad servants are not punished but seem rather to do better as such than they might have as good servants. In the former case the gain is somewhat amusing, but in the second instance it is quite lethal. But it is with the Vineyard Workers that this group reaches its clearest and most complete reversal of the preceding situations in Group A. Good servants do not get what they expected, while bad servants get more than they deserved. The contrast is at its sharpest between the normalcy of the Talents in Group A and the surprise of the Vineyard Workers in Group B.

At this point it is clear already that something rather disturbing is happening to the theme of the master-servant relationship and its moment of reckoning. If we are dealing with a constant and coherent and consistent world in which good is rewarded and bad punished and in which one knows clearly one from the other, the former group of parables stand well in their complacency. But this new group brings this very complacency and order and world into question. It is all very well to tell parables in which servants must recognize their situation and act accordingly as long as it is clear what such prudent activity entails and what is good and bad, reward and punishment, to begin with. In this sense Jesus is upsetting and undermining the conventions and expectations of his own theme. E. D. Hirsch has quoted the comment of Schleiermacher with approval: " 'Uniqueness in speech shows itself as a deviation from the characteristics that determine the genre.' " In the present case Jesus has created his own expectation and then deviated from it into polar reversal. The parables in Group B can now be seen in the light of these comments.

(a) The Unmerciful Servant. The story is only present in Matt. 18:-23–38. The full text will not be given, but certain key sections will be cited in the analysis. In its present position in Matthew the parable forms the climax of what W. G. Thompson has called in 17:22—18:35, "Matthew's advice to a divided community." Its Matthean function is easy to see: if they do not forgive their brethren, God will withdraw his forgiveness from them. Whatever may be its practical and tactical value within a disturbed community, its content is somewhat more problematic when it is abstracted from this context and taken as a basic statement about God. It is one thing to advise forgiveness of others on the model of God's forgiveness of us. We already have Matt. 5:44–45: "Love your enemies and pray for those who persecute you, so that you may be sons of your Father who is in heaven; for he makes his sun rise on the evil and on the good, and sends rain on the just and on the unjust." It is not the same thing to state as emphatically as does this parable in its present position that God will not forgive us our unforgiveness. One might wonder, minimally, if God is not also bound by the ideal of the preceding Matt. 18:21–22: "Then Peter came up and said to him, 'Lord, how often shall my brother sin against me, and I forgive him? As many as seven times?' Jesus said to him, 'I do not say to you seven times, but seventy times seven.' " It is not at all obvious how the succeeding parable is a good illustration of that saying of Jesus!

The parable itself is a small masterpiece of dramatic choreography in three tightly integrated scenes:

	Scene 1	Scene 2	Scene 3
Introduction:	18:23–25	18:28	18:31
Words:	18:26	18:29	18:32–33
Action:	18:27	18:30	18:34

The precise literary economy of this structure can be noted at three main points. First, the three scenes are bound closely together by the introductory situation of each. It starts with *master* and servant in 18:23–25: "a king wished to settle accounts with his servants. When he began the reckoning, one was brought to him. . . ." It continues with this servant and his fellow servant in 18:28: "But that same servant, as he went out, came upon one of his fellow servants. . . ." It concludes with the fellow servants and the *master* in 18:31: "When his fellow servants saw what had taken place, they were greatly distressed, and they went and reported to their lord all that had taken place." Second, the words in which the first servant pleads with his master for mercy in 18:26 are almost verbatim those used later by the second servant asking him for patience in 18:29: "So the servant fell on his knees, imploring him, 'Lord, have patience with me, and I will pay you everything' " and then, "So his fellow servant fell down and besought him, 'Have patience with me, and I will pay you.' " This agreement in the language of the plea serves to emphasize dramatically the divergent reactions to the plea in each case. In 18:27 it is: "And out of pity for him the lord of that servant released him and forgave him the debt." But in 18:30: "He refused and went and put him in prison till he should pay the debt." Third, the conclusion in 18:32–34 is especially appropriate from a dramatic and literary point of view. Since the reaction in 18:30 (nonforgiveness) was not modeled on that in 18:27 (forgiveness), then, conversely, 18:27 will be remodeled on 18:30. So 18:32–34 reads: "Then his lord summoned him and said to him, 'You wicked servant! I forgave you all that debt because you besought me; and should not you have had mercy on your fellow servant, as I had mercy on you?' And in anger his lord delivered him to the jailers [torturers], till he should pay all his debt."

Apart from the concluding verse 18:35, "So also my heavenly Father will do to every one of you, if you do not forgive your brother from your heart," in which Matthew interprets the parable for his context, the dramatic unity of the story is flawless. It shows no signs of internal thematic changes. The ordinary human reaction to such a story would be that the first servant got what he deserved and should certainly have known better in such a situation. The emphasis is not on the master's mercy but on the servant's lack of mercy and on his sheer stupidity in displaying his lack in such a way at such a time.

(b) The Servant's Reward. The text is found only in Luke 17:7–10 and reads:

"(7) Will any one of you, who has a servant plowing or keeping sheep, say to him when he has come in from the field, 'Come at once and sit down at table'? (8) Will he not rather say to him, 'Prepare supper for me, and gird yourself and serve me, till I eat and drink; and afterward you shall eat and drink'? (9) Does he thank the servant because he did what was commanded? (10) So you also, when you have done all that is commanded you, say, 'We are unworthy servants; we have only done what was our duty.' "

The basic problem is whether there is a real *parable* in 17:7–9 and its application in 17:10 or whether we are actually dealing with a *proverb* in 17:7 or 17:7, 9, which has been expanded by traditional or redactional commentary in 17:8 and 10. The discussion can be given here in summary form because its outcome does not change the main point of the unit. Be it proverb or parable, short or long, it is a flat contradiction of the logic of Group A of the Servant Parables.

Three things should be noted concerning 17:7–9. First, the parable begins with the words "will any one of you . . . ?" (or, "which one of you will . . . ?"). All the examples in the New Testament of sayings which begin with this type of interrogative format expect a firmly negative answer. The hearer is expected to be shaking one's head at the end and saying: Nobody! An example is the parable of the Friend at Midnight in Luke 11:5–8. It begins with this standard format in 11:5: "Which of you . . . ?" If a friend came to you in need at such a time of night and you were quite reasonably reluctant to be bothered, but he kept on importuning you, "which of you" would not get up and give him what he wanted, if not from friendship then at least for peace? Nobody!

Second, such questions have a general formal pattern which contains:

Situation, Circumstances, and Action. Although the line of demarcation between these elements is not always absolutely clear in the shorter sayings, these three moments are usually distinguishable. For example, this sequence is evident in Matt. 12:11 = Luke 14:5. There is the Situation: " 'What man of you, if he has one sheep." Then the Circumstances: "and it falls into a pit on the sabbath." Finally, the Action: "will not lay hold of it and lift it out?' "

Third, the New Testament examples of this question format are either in single style or else in double and parallel usage. An example of the single form is Matt. 6:27 = Luke 12:25: " 'And which of you by being anxious can add one cubit to his span of life?' " An instance of parallel form is in Matt. 7:9–10 = Luke 11:11–12: " 'Or what man of you, if his son asks him for bread, will give him a stone? Or if he asks for a fish, will give him a serpent?' "

When Luke 17:7–9 is placed against this formal background there are two obvious anomalies. First, there are two questions in 17:7 and 9 which expect the answer: Nobody would! Yet the intervening question in 17:8 breaks the format and expects the answer: Yes! This change from expected negative to positive response makes it unlikely that 17:8 was originally part of this unit. But second, even the parallelism between 17:7 and 17:9 is problematic. The former verse is longer and much more concrete, a parable in miniature. But the latter is short and abstract. It is not at all the type of parallelism for these questions just cited, for example, from Matt. 7:9–10. The most probable solution to all this is that Luke 17:7 was an original proverb of Jesus which has been gradually expanded into a short homily. For our present purpose, however, the important point is that 17:7 undermines the entire logic of those parables in which good servants are rewarded and bad servants punished. No matter how much or how little of 17:7–9 comes from Jesus, it is clear that Group A has been contradicted.

(c) The Unjust Steward. The parable appears only in Luke 16:1–7 and can be given in full:

" '(1) There was a rich man who had a steward, and charges were brought to him that this man was wasting his goods. (2) And he called him and said to him, 'What is this that I hear about you? Turn in the account of your stewardship, for you can no longer be steward.' (3) And the steward said to himself, 'What shall I do, since my master is taking the stewardship away from me? I am not strong enough to dig, and I am ashamed to beg. (4) I have decided what to do, so that people may receive me into their houses when I am put out of the stewardship.' (5) So, summoning his master's debtors one by one, he said to the first, 'How much do you owe my master?' (6) He said, 'A hundred measures of oil.' And he said to him, 'Take your bill, and sit down quickly and write fifty.' (7) Then he said to another, 'And how much do you owe?' He said, 'A hundred measures of wheat.' He said to him, 'Take your bill, and write eighty.' "

There is already a scholarly consensus that a variety of applications have been added to this parable in the succeeding verses in Luke 16:-8–13. The classical statement of this is in C. H. Dodd: "We can almost see here notes for three separate sermons on the parable as text." But this consensus breaks down completely when one discusses where the original parable ended and the additions began. Scholars have argued for an original ending at 16:9 or 16:8b or 16:8a or 16:7 as given here. There are two obvious objections to taking the parable as a model of almsgiving and ending it with 16:8b or 16:9; "for the sons of this world are wiser in their own generation than the sons of light. And I tell you, make friends for yourselves by means of unrighteous mammon, so that when it fails they may receive you into the eternal habitations." If it is the master's money, should one give alms from another's property? And if it is not the master's money but the steward's exorbitant profits which are being reduced, is it alms to reduce large amounts of usury to smaller ones? The problem with 16:8a as the original ending is equally well known. If the "master" is the rich man of the parable, is it really likely he would have praised the steward? And if the "master" means Jesus, we are already out of the parable and into commentary. Hence, in this study, the parable will be taken as ending originally at 16:7.

Some recent studies have argued that the steward was not doing anything unjust in 16:5–7 but was simply reducing his own usurious profits within the agency which the master had farmed out to him. This may well be true and would probably not change the central thrust of the story in any case, but it does not pay sufficient attention to 16:2 within the literary economy of the story. Whatever is happening in 16:5–7 there was already a problem between master and servant as early as 16:2 ("wasting his goods"). When 16:2 and 16:5–7 are read together *within* the literary tension of the story, one has a picture of laziness organizing itself under crisis. The steward has not obtained sufficient return for the master and is therefore being removed (16:2). In such a situation he may as well get some terminal benefits from the master's losses and so ingratiates himself with the debtors (16:5–7). When he is later out of a job they will, hopefully, feel grateful to him for his help and maybe even responsible for his firing (16:3–4). He has created a sort of Robin Hood image out of his inefficiency.

The parable is a carefully formed mini-drama in 16:1–7. It is as elegantly structured as was that of the Unmerciful Servant and is constructed in three scenes each of which is an internal diptych:

Scene 1 (16:1–2): Master and Steward
    (a) 16:1a   (relationship given: 16:2a   (accusation repeated:
                  "steward")   "I hear")
    (b) 16:1b   (accusation made: 16:2b   (relationship broken:
                  "charges")   "no longer")
Scene 2 (16:3–4): Steward and Self
    (a) 16:3a = 16:4a ("What shall I do"/"I have decided what to do")
    (b) 16:3b = 16:4b ("stewardship"/"stewardship")
    (c) 16:3c = 16:4c (problem/solution)
Scene 3 (16:5–7): Steward and Debtors
    (a) 16:5a = 16:7a ("he said to the first"/"he said to another")
    (b) 16:5b = 16:7b ("how much do you owe?" in both cases)
    (c) 16:6a = 16:7c ("He said, 'A hundred' " in both cases)
    (d) 16:6b = 16:7d ("Take your bill . . . and write" in both cases)

The construction is quite clear and only a few comments are needed on Scene 1 in 16:1–2. The chiastic structure of this unit is important in setting up both the problem and the avenue of solution: " 'Turn in the account of your stewardship, for you can no longer be steward.' " In such a situation one might as well be hung for a sheep as a lamb. The steward *is* dismissed for incompetence and yet is allowed to set up the "accounting" at which he has nothing to lose and everything to gain by further but calculated incompetence. The cleverness of the steward consisted not only in solving his problem but in solving it by means of the very reason (low profits) that had created it in the first place. In the light of all this the parable ends quite adequately at 16:7. The rest, including 16:8a, is commentary. Once again, however, Group A is being challenged. A bad servant, from both 16:2 and 16:5–7, is not really punished for being such. In fact it seems to be rather profitable. It is no wonder that the tradition, from as early as 16:8a, was a little shocked by this parable.

(d) The Wicked Husbandmen. This parable has already been studied quite fully in an earlier section. When its best version is taken as that in Gos. Thom. 93:1–15, the story is very similar to that of the Unjust Steward. Both tell stories of immoral action in which bad servants are not punished but seem rather to prevail by increased evil. The tradition had solved all this by moralizing the Unjust Steward as a model for almsgiving and by allegorizing the Wicked Husbandmen as the sequence of salvation history, but with only partial success in each case. Indeed, what J. Jeremias said of the Unjust Steward might apply to both these parables: "The shock, much discussed, naturally produced by a parable which seems to present a criminal as a pattern disappears when we consider the parable in its original form. . . . Jesus is apparently dealing with an actual case which had been indignantly related to him. He deliberately took it as an example, knowing that it would secure redoubled attention. . . . They would expect that Jesus would end the story with an expression of strong disapproval, instead of which, to their surprise, Jesus praises the criminal. . . . he recognized the critical nature of the situation. . . . he acted, unscrupulously no doubt . . . but boldly, resolutely, and prudently, with the purpose of making a new life for himself."

(e) The Vineyard Workers. The parable is found only in Matt. 20:-1–13. Because of its importance it must be given in full:

" 'For the kingdom of heaven is like a householder who went out early in the morning to hire laborers for his vineyard. After agreeing with the laborers for a denarius a day, he sent them into his vineyard. And going out about the third hour he saw others standing idle in the market place; and to them he said, "You go into the vineyard too, and whatever is right I will give you." So they went. Going out again about the sixth and the ninth hour, he did the same. And about the eleventh hour he went out and found others standing; and he said to them, "Why do you stand here idle all day?" They said to him, "Because no one has hired us." He said to them, "You go into the vineyard too." And when evening came, the owner of the vineyard said to his steward, "Call the laborers and pay them their wages, beginning with the last, up to the first." And when those hired about the eleventh hour came, each of them received a denarius. Now when the first came, they thought they would receive more; but each of them also received a denarius. And on receiving it they grumbled at the householder, saying, "These last worked only one hour, and you have made them equal to us who have borne the burden of the day and scorching heat." But he replied to one of them, "Friend, I am doing you no wrong; did you not agree with me for a denarius?" ' "

The first question is to decide where exactly did the original parable end. There is a consensus that 20:16, " 'So the last will be first, and the first last,' " does not belong to the original parable. The basic reason is that it is repeated here from Matt. 19:30, the immediately preceding section, and that 19:30 is taken from Mark 10:31. But most scholars have accepted 20:1–15 as the basic original story. It is argued here that the original parable ended with the rhetorical question of 20:13, and this will be of some importance for the interpretation. Actually, it would make little interpretive difference if 20:14, " 'Take what belongs to you, and go; I choose to give to this last as I give to you,' " were original but the presence or absence of 20:15 is crucial. This verse reads: " 'Am I not allowed to do what I choose with what belongs to me? Or do you begrudge my generosity [*literally:* is your eye evil because I am good]?' " The contrast of "eye evil" (see Mark 7:22 and Matt. 6:23) and "I am good" has necessarily brought moral considerations into the very climax of the parable itself, and the commentators rely heavily on 20:15 for their interpretation and application of this parable. Some examples of 20:15 as the key to the parable's meaning make this very evident. C. H. Dodd speaks of the "employer, out of sheer generosity and compassion for the unemployed . . . a striking picture of the divine generosity." J. Jeremias says that "God is depicted as acting like an employer who has compassion for the unemployed and their families." E. Linnemann comments that "The master of the house is able, however, to show that justice has been satisfied: what appeared as a breach in the ordered system of justice was in truth the appearance of goodness, and goodness cannot be disapproved." But for the following four reasons, 20:15 must be considered as a Matthean addition to the original parable.

First, the language. The combination of "good" and "evil" is present in all but one of Matthew's uses of the term "good." So Matt. 5:45; 7:11, 17–18; 12:34–35; 22:10; 25:21, 23, 26. This combination, present also here in Matt. 20:15, is not typically characteristic of Mark (see, for example, 3:4) or Luke (see, for example, 8:8, 15). Indeed, the very use of the term "evil" is predominatly Matthean in the New Testament. He uses it as much as Mark, Luke, John, and Acts put together.

Second, the context. There is a close contextual and conceptual relationship between Matt. 19:16–30, the story of the rich man, and Matt. 20:1–15, which immediately follows it. This shows up most explicitly in the repetition of 19:30 in 20:16 (last first, first last). In Mark 10:17–18 =Luke 18:18–19 Jesus was addressed by the rich man as: " 'Good Teacher,' " and he refused this title with the comment, " 'Why do you call me good? No one is good but God alone.' " Matt. 19:16–17, in taking over this unit from Mark, was not at all happy with this refusal and he performed a careful restatement on Mark's text. Jesus is now addressed simply as " 'Teacher,' " and he answers, " 'Why do you ask me about what is good? One there is who is good.' " In other words, for Matthew, Jesus does not refuse the title of "good" and the phrase " 'One there is who is good' " might even include himself as God's delegate. The reason for this becomes evident at the end of our parable in 20:15. It is the "good" Jesus of 19:17 who will return as Son of Man in 19:28 and will dispense judgment as the "I am good" of 20:15. Thus, 20:15 is a Matthean recapitulation of 19:17 and is intended to bind the parable more firmly into its present contextual position and meaning.

Third, the concepts. It is not at all so evident that the action of the master is "good." It is certainly not unjust (20:13 = 2), but most normal people would not call it good except in a rather perverse way. He would be good and generous if, having given the last hired one denarius, he had increased the pay proportionately for all the others.

Fourth, aesthetics. Not only is a rhetorical question a very good ending for a parable since it draws the hearer more deeply into the parabolic world, but the question of 20:3, " 'I am doing you no wrong; did you not agree with me for a denarius?' " explicitly recalls the opening commitments of 20:2, 4, "after agreeing with the laborers for a denarius a day . . . what is right I will give you.' " This concludes the story both logically and dramatically. Thus 20:15 must be removed from the original version and, most likely, so also should 20:14. Its function was probably to prepare for 20:15. Note the "I choose" in 20:14 and 20:15.

Once again we can draw attention to the careful construction of 20:1–13. There are two scenes differentiated by the balance of the initial 20:1, "early," in 20:1–7, and the opening 20:8, "evening," of 20:8–13.

In the former scene five groups are hired but only three groups receive any emphasis, and the vocabulary contacts already indicate this: compare 20:2–4 with 20:7. This also serves to close off the unity of the first scene as 20:1–7. The second scene opens in 20:8 in what looks like expected harmony with 20:1. But 20:8b introduces already an unexpected note: " 'beginning with the last, up to the first.' " This already points to the reversal of expectations which ensues in 20:9–13, and it also cuts down the groups under discussion to two: the last and the first. The rest are forgotten. The reversal can be diagrammed as follows:

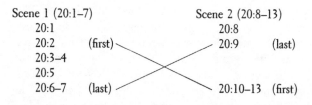

Scene 1 (20:1–7)   Scene 2 (20:8–13)
    20:1   20:8
    20:2   (first)   20:9   (last)
    20:3–4
    20:5
    20:6–7   (last)   20:10–13   (first)

The reversal is highlighted by a comparison with the Talents in Matt. 25:14–30. There the sequence is always the good servants first and then the bad servant, in all the three scenes. The Vineyard Workers followed this order in the first scene but reversed it in the second one.

The story told by Jesus went out of its way to avoid the intrusion of morality. There is no injustice on the part of the master (20:2, 4, 13) and there is no laziness to be punished on the part of the servants (20:6–7). Can one imagine a perfectly reasonable situation in which perfectly reasonable expectations are rudely overthrown? The owner is *not* one who is especially generous but one who violates expectations. There could be no *total* reversal of salary without the point of the parable slipping out of focus. The owner does not pay the first the least and the last the most. In that story the hearer would have to wonder at the clear "injustice" of such an action. Jesus must create a story which is quite possible and which does not raise irrelevant moral considerations. It is reversal of expectation which is central: "they thought" in 20:10. D. O. Via summed up the parable with this: "Our very existence depends on whether we will accept God's gracious dealings, his dealings which shatter our calculations about how things ought to be ordered in the world." But God also shatters our understanding of graciousness and that is the most difficult of all to accept. What comes across most forcibly within our present purpose is that this parable shatters utterly the normalcy of Group A and brings to a climax the drive of Group B of the Servant Parables.

(4) The Structure of the Reversal. For the purpose of the present analysis we shall concentrate on the eight Servant parables and leave aside the Servant proverb in Luke 17:7. The purpose is to see how the reversal of the theme's development is reflected in the structure of the two groups of Servant parables.

(a) The Structure in Group A. The four parables of this group move within the horizon of expected normalcy: good servants are rewarded and bad ones punished. This normalcy of world is reflected in a very marked homogeneity of structure. This homogeneity can be indicated under three rubrics: development, elements, expansion.

First, development. The common theme of both groups is the master-servant relationship at a moment of critical reckoning. To develop this image into story one could take the binary opposition of departure/ return and then go in one of two rather obvious ways. Either the master departs and returns later to see what the servant has done or not done in his absence, or the servant departs and then returns to report to the master what he has done or not done. Group A all follow the former possibility: the master goes and returns. Group B all go the alternative route. It is ironically amusing that Group A which details a departing and returning master and which was so dear to the early church's expectation of the returning Son of Man, their master Jesus, was already undermined by Jesus in Group B which focuses on a departing and returning servant.

Second, the elements. The basic pattern, then, is a departing and returning master. Within this pattern, the choice and sequence of elements are also remarkably homogeneous. In Group A the structural elements are: Command, Departure, Activity, Return, Reward and/or Punishment.

Third, expansion. Despite this homogeneity of thematic development and elemental sequence, variety is still present in the four parables of Group A because of a process of expansion from the Doorkeeper, where the reward and the punishment is implicit, to the Throne Claimant, where the bad are punished, to the Overseer, where good is rewarded *or* bad is punished, and finally to the Talents, where both the good is rewarded *and* the bad is punished. This last parable brings this development to its fullest form and most careful construction.

(b) The Structure in Group B. There are two major structural differences between Group A and Group B. In Group A normalcy of world was reflected in harmony of structure and homogeneity of development. In Group B the questioning of this normalcy is reflected in the total lack of structural homogeneity. Each of the four parables in Group B is carefully constructed within its own closed unity but there is no common pattern or sequence of elements discernible across all four of them. In other words, as soon as the normalcy of world in Group A is questioned by Group B, the structural homogeneity of Group A disappears and no other structural harmony appears within Group B itself.

The second major difference is that these parables develop their theme in the second and opposite possibility to that in Group A. Now the servant departs and then returns to the master to report. The Unmerciful Servant is called in before his master: "one was brought to him" in Matt. 18:24. The Unjust Steward is also called in to the master: "he called him" in Luke 16:2. The Wicked Husbandmen is more complicated. The master here is an absentee landlord and not a departing and returning master. The messengers serve here the function of bringing the tenants' rent before the master. In Gos. Thom. 93:1–2, "A good man had a vineyard. He gave it to husbandmen," there is no mention of a departing master. This appears only in Mark 12:1, "and went into another country," which is the same phrase used by Mark 13:34 to open his parable of the Doorkeeper. So also, at the close of the Wicked Husbandmen in Mark 12:9 the owner returns: "the owner . . . will come." There is nothing about this in the Gospel of Thomas, as seen earlier. In other words, the synoptic tradition is trying to move this parable into the more usual pattern of the departing and returning master from Group A. Finally, in the Vineyard Workers it is again the servants who depart and return to the master: "he sent them" in 20:2; "go" in 20:4, 7; and then "Call the laborers" in 20:8.

(c) Comparative Structure of the Groups. It is now clear that these Servant parables might also be termed parables of Reckoning. The comparative structure of the two groups shows how the thematic development concludes by questioning and then reversing itself. The two structures can be outlined as follows (Rk = Reckoning; M = Master; S = Servant; R = Reward; P = Punishment; G = Good; B = Bad; d = departure; r = return):A glance at the two structures shows how they unfold

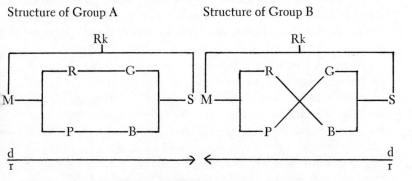

Structure of Group A   Structure of Group B

along various sets of binary opposites: MS, RP, GB, dr.

(d) Structure and Oral Tradition. For people raised in a writing culture the term "ipsissima verba" means exactly what it says. When we apply the phrase to an oral tradition we tend to presume it means precise verbal fidelity to an original version with some allowance for the limits of memory and recall. But the evidence would indicate that people who are *operating* within a tradition of oral deliverance and remembrance, even if there is also a tradition of writing available in their culture, may even use a term such as "ipsissima verba" where they actually mean what we would call "ipsissima structura." A. B. Lord has shown how Yugoslav poet-singers working in an epic tradition of oral narrative poetry claim they can hear and repeat thousands of lines "word for word." But when one hears and reads such a "repetition" it is a creative act of fidelity to the basic story with its general structure and sequence of elements and not at all a case of "ipsissima verba."

This raises the following questions concerning the parables of Jesus as the compositions of an oral poet. Could it be that Jesus told the parable of the Talents, for example, over and over again with minor variations within the same general content and structure? The tradition might then have preserved two or more such individual tellings. This has been suggested by R. W. Funk: "It is more accurate, therefore, to speak of independent traditions rather than of an original parable." In most cases, however, when one compares independent versions of a parable, one is usually constrained to take one over another as "more original," that is, as closer to that which is taken as coming from the historical Jesus. One seldom ends up with two or more equally good variations. There is, however, another way of formulating this question. Could it be that the tradition preserved originally not any concrete ("authentic") telling but a structural outline or skeletal story? In other words, when traditional and redactional layers are removed from the Talents, for example, is what remains as the "original" version the structural outline of a multiform and many-times-told parable of the historical Jesus? This might be defended by quoting A. B. Lord's apodictic statement: "In oral tradition the idea of an original is illogical." But this presumes that the *only* type of oral poetry is epic narrative which is metrical, musical, and very traditional in story, theme, and formula. It presumes that the Homeric bards and the Yugoslav singers are the only oral poets around. It must be noted, to the contrary, that Jesus' parables are neither metrical nor musical and hence have no necessity for fixed formulaic patterns. They are short and dramatic rather than long and epic. And, as we have tried to show throughout this book, these parables are antitraditional in intention. Hence one must question very strongly the absolute formulation of A. B. Lord: "oral poets who are not traditional do not exist."

But it is especially the data of the Servant parables that argues for a negative answer to this question concerning multiform versions of the same parable. In these parables, at least, Jesus' creativity shows itself in two ways. First, there are major changes of content within the same structure: see Group A. Second, there are major changes of structure within the same theme: see Group B. But we have no direct evidence that Jesus makes minor changes of detail within the same story content. We do not really know how often or if ever again Jesus worked with so many parables within the same theme as in the Servant case, so it may be dangerous to extrapolate from this one rather striking case. But we do know that the primitive community had obvious reasons for preserving the theme of the master-servant relationship and its crisis of reckoning, so it is quite likely that we have this one case preserved not because it was the only one of its kind but because it was the one most wanted for retention by the tradition. In so far as we can legitimately generalize from the case of the Servant parables, then, it would seem that the parabolic creativity of Jesus consisted in variations of structure within the same theme and in variations of content within the same structure *but not* in variations of detail within the same content. No doubt it took such a restless probing of structure to express adequately the challenge Jesus was offering to his tradition. It was only through such constant variety in his parables that Jesus could render visible the structure of the Kingdom's temporality which was their theme. As C. Lévi-Strauss has noted concerning myths: "the question has often been raised why myths, and more generally oral literature, are so much addicted to duplication, triplication, or quadruplication of the same sequence. . . . The function of repetition is to render the structure of the myth apparent."

(5) The Interpretation of the Structure. It is now possible to draw some interpretive conclusions from all this. The reversal within the parabolic theme of the Servants represents another example of what was seen earlier in the parables of reversal themselves. It was noted in that section that there are certain paradoxical proverbs of Jesus and a whole group of parables which are linguistic attempts to shatter the complacency of one's world in the name of the Kingdom's advent. This is an even wider example of this same linguistic eschatology. Here it is not a short proverb or even a long parable which is in question. It is an entire parabolic theme which is developed in one set of parables (Group A) and then reversed and overthrown in another (Group B). We do not know how many such parables were originally given by Jesus. Only eight are extant in the synoptic tradition. The Gospel of Thomas did not find them too congenial and has preserved only one, the Wicked Husbandmen, from the whole series.

The parables of action all challenge one to life and action in response to the Kingdom's advent. But the Servant parable introduces a very disturbing note into all this. The temporality of the Kingdom appears in the three simultaneous modes of advent, reversal, and action. But as advent takes priority over reversal so does this latter over action. In the eight parables of the Servant cluster a theme is presented in ordered normalcy and then is just as carefully reversed and shattered. Like a wise and prudent servant calculating what he must do in the critical reckoning to which his master summons him, one must be ready and willing to respond in life and action to the eschatological advent of God. But, unfortunately, the eschatological advent of God will always be precisely that for which wise and prudent readiness is impossible because it shatters also our wisdom and our prudence.

CONCLUSION: THIRTEEN WAYS OF LOOKING AT A PARABLE

O yes, technique—but much more:
the god still is balanced
                          in the man-stones.
    but it's a nice thing
as near a thing as ever you saw.
        (David Jones, *The Anathemata*, p. 94)

One is artist if one experiences as *content*, as the "thing itself," that which all nonartists call "form." In so doing one belongs without a doubt to a crazy world: for from now on all content appears as purely formal—our lives included.
        (F. Nietzsche, in H. Birault, *On Heidegger and Language*, p. 153)

I am happy and I think full of an energy, of an energy I had despaired of. It seems to me that I have found what I wanted. When I try to put all into a phrase I say, "Man can embody truth but he cannot know it." I must embody it in the completion of my life. The abstract is not life and everywhere draws out its contradictions. You can refute Hegel but not the Saint or the Song of Sixpence.
        (W. B. Yeats, last letter, in J. H. Miller, *Poets of Reality*, p. 125)

Metaphor is as ultimate as speech itself, and speech as ultimate as thought. If we try to penetrate them beyond a certain point, we find ourselves questioning the very faculty and instrument with which we are trying to penetrate them.
        (J. M. Murry, in W. A. Shibles, *Metaphor*, p. 200)

so much depends
upon

a red wheel
barrow
      (W. C. Williams, "Spring and All," *Collected Earlier Poems*, p. 277)

Even more disconcerting is the vanishing of metaphor, in the old conception. Metaphor is there all right, but exploded to page size, so big we do not perceive it as a trope, organic or ornamental, but undergo it as drama.
      (D. Mus, on "The Waste Land," *Poetry*, 121 (1972), p. 158)

These highest peaks of self, when the largest areas of the vague unconscious are brought to an intensity of consciousness, when the whole potential of humanity seems realized in the individual, cannot be analyzed or explained but only experienced and, if the artist's faith is justified, perhaps re-experienced in metaphors and symbols: in autobiography and poetry.
      (James Olney, *Metaphors of Self*, p. 25)

THE WORLD IS COMING

high and wide, in the vacant air . . .

straight throught the four white walls of the real

until it no longer appears

different

from what the eye sees.
      (Ronald Johnson, "Poem," *Poetry*, 120 (1972), p. 144)

The theorist of poetry tends more and more today to make metaphor the irreducible element of his definition of poetry, but in attempting to define metaphor itself he tends furthermore to shoot off into an endlessly interesting series of metaphors.
      (W. K. Wimsatt, Jr., *The Verbal Icon*, p. 128)

For Barthes a language and a style are "objects," while a mode of *écriture* (writing, personal utterance) is a "function." Neither strictly historical nor irredeemably personal, *écriture* occupies a middle ground; it is "essentially the morality of form." In contrast to a language and a style, *écriture* is the writer's zone of freedom, "form considered as human intention."
      (Susan Sontag, on Roland Barthes, *Writing Degree Zero*, pp. xvii–xviii)

It is the artist . . . who first clearly and fully discovers and presents to us through his creative gifts the values and the meanings by which we live. He gives us our world: a world which is later structured in a systematic way by theory, including the interpretations of philosophy and science, as well as those of religion and morality.

(E. Vivas, *The Artistic Transaction*, p. 17)

This is why it would not be wrong to consider this book itself as a myth: it is, as it were, the myth of mythology.

(C. Lévi-Strauss, *The Raw and the Cooked*, p. 12)

Thanks for the evening; but how
Shall we satisfy when we meet
Between Shall-I and I-Will,
The lion's mouth whose hunger
No metaphors can Fill?

(W. H. Auden, *Collected Longer Poems*, p. 202)

Notes

(The numbers at the left refer to the pages of this book. When a work is cited more than once the full details will be given the first time. Thereafter abbreviations will be used.)

xiii   W. Stevens, *The Collected Poems of Wallace Stevens* (New York: Knopf, 1954), p. 322.

xiv   F. Kafka, *Parables and Paradoxes* (New York: Schocken, (1961), p. 11.

W. C. Williams, "Asphodel, that Greeny Flower," in *Pictures from Brueghel and Other Poems* (Norfolk, Conn.: New Directions, 1962), p. 179.

xv   Stevens, "Asides on the Oboe," *Collected Poems*, p. 250.

W. H. Auden, "For the Time Being," *Collected Longer Poems* (New York: Random House, 1969), p. 175.

R. Barthes, "Historical Discourse," *Introduction to Structuralism*, ed. M. Lane (New York: Basic Books, 1970), p. 155.

W. Heisenberg, cited by W. H. Auden, *Secondary Worlds* (New York: Random House, 1968), p. 143.

J. Giraudoux, *Tiger at the Gates*, tr. Christopher Fry (New York: Oxford University Press, 1955), p. 32.

M. Heidegger, "Remembrance of the Poet," *Existence and Being*, ed. W. Brock (Chicago: Regnery, 1949), pp. 234–235.

xvi   E. Pound, "Canto 80," cited in C. Brooke-Rose, *A ZBC of Ezra Pound* (Berkeley & Los Angeles: University of California Press, 1971), p. 13.

4   Stevens, *Collected Poems*, p. 15.

9   Goethe, cited in E. Kahler, "The Nature of the Symbol," *Symbolism in Religion and Literature*, ed. R. May (New York: Braziller, 1960), pp. 70–71.

W. B. Yeats, *Essays and Introductions* (New York: Macmillan, 1961), p. 147.

Coleridge, cited in L. C. Knights, "Idea and Symbol: Some Hints from Coleridge,"

Metaphor and Symbol, eds., L. C. Knights & B. Cottle (London: Butterworths, 1960), p. 135.

10   T. S. Eliot, "Introduction," to *All Hollows' Eve* by Charles Williams (New York: Pellegrini & Cudahy, 1948), p. xiv.

11   L. Wittgenstein, *Tractatus Logico-Philosophicus* (London: Routledge & Kegan Paul, 1922), in "Preface" and #7.

H. Rago, "The Vocation of Poetry," *Poetry*, 110 (1967), pp. 328–348; "The Poet in His Poem," *Poetry*, 113 (1969), pp. 413–420. See, respectively, pp. 340, 414, 415.

P. Ricoeur, *The Symbolism of Evil* (Boston: Beacon, 1969), pp. 163–164.

12   H. Kenner, *The Poetry of Ezra Pound* (Norfolk, Conn.: New Directions, 1968), p. 195.

C. Brooks, "Metaphor and the Function of Criticism," *Spiritual Problems in Contemporary Literature*, ed. S. R. Hopper (Gloucester, Mass.: Peter Smith, 1969), pp. 127–137.

C. S. Lewis, "Bluspels and Flalansferes," *The Importance of Language*, ed. M. Black (Ithaca, N.Y.: Cornell University Press, 1969), pp. 36–50. The essay dates from 1939.

13   Pound, "Canto 87," cited in *ZBC*, p. 206.

Stevens, *Collected Poems*, pp. 16, 94, and *Opus Posthumous* (New York: Knopf, 1957), p. 19, respectively.

H. Marcuse, *One-Dimensional Man* (Boston: Beacon, 1964), p. 192.

14   M. Foucault, *The Order of Things* (New York: Pantheon, 1970), p. xviii.

Fenollosa, cited in H. Kenner, *The Pound Era* (Berkeley & Los Angeles: University of California Press, 1971), p. 119.

Eliot, cited also in *The Pound Era*, p. 31. See also T. S. Eliot, "A Commentary," *Criterion*, 12 (1932), pp. 73–79.

15   W. Stevens, *The Necessary Angel* (New York: Knopf, 1951), p. 32.

O. Barfield, *Poetic Diction: A Study in Meaning* (2nd ed.; London: Faber & Faber, 1952); "Poetic Diction and Legal Fiction," *The Importance of Language*, pp. 51–57; *Saving the Appearances: A Study in Idolatry* (New York: Harcourt, Brace & World, 1957); "The Meaning of the Word 'Literal,'" *Metaphor and Symbol*, pp. 48–63.

M. Moore, *Collected Poems* (New York: Macmillan, 1951), p. 41. These lines from "Poetry" were omitted from *The Complete Poems of Marianne Moore* (New York: Macmillan/Viking, 1967), p. 36.

16   R. West, cited in M. H. Abrams, *The Mirror and the Lamp* (New York: Oxford University Press, 1953), p. 100.

T. S. Eliot, *On Poetry and Poets* (New York: Farrar, Straus & Cudahy, 1957), p. 94.

A. Tate, "The Symbolic Imagination: The Mirrors of Dante," *The New Orpheus: Essays Toward a Christian Poetic* (New York: Sheed & Ward, 1964), p. 99.

S. Nodelman, "Structural analysis in art and anthropology," *Structuralism*, ed. J. Ehrmann (New York: Doubleday, 1970 = *Yale French Studies*, 36–37 [1966]), p. 92.

17   W. B. Yeats in a letter to Katharine Tynan, cited in N. Jeffares, *W. B. Yeats: Man and Poet* (New York: Barnes & Noble, 1966), pp. 41–42.

W. B. Yeats, "Adam's Curse," *The Collected Poems of W. B. Yeats* (New York: Macmillan, 1956), pp. 78–79.

T. S. Eliot, "The Four Quartets: Little Gidding," *The Complete Poems and Plays* (New York: Harcourt, Brace & Co., 1952), p. 145.

18   Yeats, as cited in Jeffares, *Man and Poet*, p. 38.

M. Merleau-Ponty, as cited in R. W. Funk, *Language, Hermeneutic, and Word of God* (New York: Harper & Row, 1966), p. 123.

N. Frye, *Anatomy of Criticism* (New York: Atheneum, 1970), pp. 27–28.

19   T. Fawcett, *The Symbolic Language of Religion* (London: SCM Press, 1970), pp. 170–171.

Sukkah 2:9, in H. Danby, *The Mishnah* (London: Oxford University Press, 1933), p. 175.

20   Example is cited from N. Perrin, *Rediscovering the Teaching of Jesus* (London: SCM Press, 1967), p. 84.

21   G. Bornkamm, *Jesus of Nazareth* (New York: Harper & Row, 1960), p. 69.

P. Ricoeur, "The Symbol—Food for Thought," *Philosophy Today*, 4 (1960), pp. 196–207.

22   E. Erikson, *Young Man Luther* (New York: Norton, 1958), p. 35.

Fawcett, *Symbolic Language*, p. 170.

23   Perrin, *Rediscovering*, pp. 54 and 55, respectively.

24   A. Schweitzer, *The Quest of the Historical Jesus* (New York: Macmillan, 1968), p. 356.

C. H. Dodd, *The Parables of the Kingdom* (rev. ed.; New York: Scribner, 1961), pp. 82–84.

J. Jeremias, *The Parables of Jesus* (rev. ed.; New York: Scribner, 1963), p. 230.

J. M. Robinson, "The Formal Structure of Jesus' Message," *Current Issues in New Testament Interpretation* ("Essays in honor of O. A. Piper"; New York: Harper & Brothers, 1962), pp. 91–110 (see 97).

25   N. Perrin, "The Composition of Mark ix,1," *Novum Testamentum*, 11 (1969), pp. 67–70.

N. Perrin, *The Kingdom of God in the Teaching of Jesus* (Philadelphia: Westminster Press, 1963), p. 185.

R. W. Funk, "Apocalyptic as an Historical and Theological Problem in Current New Testament Scholarship," *Apocalypticism* (New York: Herder & Herder = *Journal for Theology and the Church*, 6 [1969]), pp. 175–191.

26   B. Vawter, "Intimations of Immortality and the Old Testament," *Journal of Biblical Literature*, 91 (1972), pp. 158–171.

27   G. von Rad, *Old Testament Theology*, Vol. 2 (Edinburgh: Oliver & Boyd, 1965), pp. 99–102.

28   Eliot, "Four Quartets: Burnt Norton," *Complete Poems*, pp. 120–121.

29   Yeats, "The Song of the Happy Shepherd," *Collected Poems*, p. 7.

D. Laing, cited in P. Wheelwright, *The Burning Fountain* (rev. ed.; Bloomington, Ind.: Indiana University Press, 1968), p. 148.

Stevens, *Opus Posthumous*, p. 175.

S. Spender, cited in *Spiritual Problems in Contemporary Literature*, p. 1.

R. E. Palmer, *Hermeneutics* (Evanston: Northwestern University Press, 1969), p. 176.

30   D. Jones, *The Anathemata* (London: Faber & Faber, 1952), p. 170.

Auden, *Collected Longer Poems*, p. 177.

T. S. Eliot, "Four Quartets: The Dry Salvages," *Four Quartets* (New York: Harcourt, Brace & World, 1943), p. 36.

M. Ross, "The Writer as Christian," *The New Orpheus*, p. 91.

E. Pound, "Canto 92," *The Cantos (1–95)* (New York: New Directions, 1956), p. 80 (from "Section: Rock Drill").

Stevens, "The Greenest Continent," *Opus Posthumous*, p. 53.

31   T. Kisiel, "The Language of the Event: The Event of Language," *Heidegger and the Path of Thinking*, ed. J. Sallis (Pittsburgh: Duquesne University Press, 1970), pp. 85–104 (see 95).

32   Heidegger, *Existence and Being*, p. 289; and *Poetry, Language, Thought*, ed. A. Hofstadter (New York: Harper & Row, 1971), p. 4, respectively.

Jeremias, *Parables*, p. 21.

33   J. Lacan, "The insistence of the letter in the unconscious," *Structuralism*, p. 112.

C. Lévi-Strauss, *The Raw and the Cooked* (New York: Harper & Row, 1969), p. 2.

P. E. Lewis, "Merleau-Ponty and the phenomenology of language," *Structuralism*, pp. 9–31.

35   Yeats, "Two Songs from a Play," *Collected Poems*, pp. 210–211.

37   Stevens, *Collected Poems*, p. 341.

E. Pound, *Literary Essays of Ezra Pound*, ed. T. S. Eliot (London: Faber & Faber, 1954), p. 9.

N. A. Scott, *The Wild Prayer of Longing* (New Haven: Yale University Press, 1971), pp. 1–42.

43   B. H. Smith, *Poetic Closure* (Chicago: University of Chicago Press, 1968), p. 92.

46   J. R. Donahue's address, "Tradition and Redaction in the Markan Trial Narrative (Mk 14:53–65)," was given to the Catholic Biblical Association Convention, Sept. 1, 1970.

N. Perrin, "The Christology of Mark: A Study in Methodology," *Journal of Religion*, 51 (1971), pp. 173–187, noted that Donahue had found 47 instances of this in Mark.

47   J. D. Kingsbury, *The Parables of Jesus in Matthew 13* (Richmond, Va.: John Knox Press, 1969), p. 81.

48   B. H. Streeter, *The Four Gospels: A Study of Origins* (London: Macmillan, 1924), p. 187.

Jeremias, *Parables*, p. 148.

H. K. McArthur, "The Parable of the Mustard Seed," *Catholic Biblical Quarterly*, 33 (1971), pp. 198–201.

50   Tate, "The Symbolic Imagination," p. 99.

E. Käsemann, *Perspectives on Paul* (Philadelphia: Fortress Press, 1971), p. 8.

N. A. Dahl, "The Parables of Growth," *Studia Theologica*, 5 (1951), pp. 132–165.

51   Moritake, cited from *ZBC*, p. 98.

T. Roethke, *The Collected Poems of Theodore Roethke* (Garden City, N.Y.: Doubleday, 1966).

H. Hesse, *Siddhartha* (New York: New Directions, 1951), pp. 27–28.

53   Auden, *Collected Longer Poems*, p. 138.

G. Gunn, "Literature and its Relation to Religion," *Journal of Religion*, 50 (1970), pp. 268–291.

54   Kingsbury, *Matthew 13*, p. 4.

55   Kenner, *The Poetry of Ezra Pound*, p. 62.

R. Bultmann, *The History of the Synoptic Tradition* (New York: Harper & Row, 1963), pp. 169–179.

57   Jeremias, *Parables*, p. 205.

E. Linnemann, *Jesus of the Parables* (New York: Harper & Row, 1966), p. 56.

G. V. Jones, *The Art and Truth of the Parables* (London: S.P.C.K., 1964), pp. 115, 120, 154, 156, respectively.

Perrin, *Rediscovering*, pp. 123–124.

D. O. Via, *The Parables* (Philadelphia: Fortress Press, 1967), p. 12.

Dodd, *Parables*, pp. 1–2, 100.

60   Bultmann, *Synoptic Tradition*, pp. 182–183.

61   Bultmann, *Synoptic Tradition*, pp. 41–42.

67   Jeremias, *Parables*, p. 183.

70   Bultmann, *Synoptic Tradition*, p. 179.

71   R. J. Dillon, "Towards a Tradition-History of the Parables of the True Israel (Matthew 21, 33–22, 14)," *Biblica*, 47 (1966), pp. 1–42.

75   E. Pound, *ABC of Reading* (London: Routledge & Sons, 1934), p. 84.

Aristotle, Poetics 22:9 (Loeb translation), cited in *ZBC*, 95, note 3.

76   W. A. Beardslee, "Uses of the Proverb in the Synoptic Gospel," *Interpretation*, 24 (1970), pp. 61–76. See also his *Literary Criticism of the New Testament* (Philadelphia: Fortress Press, 1970), pp. 30–41; "Proverbs in the Gospel of Thomas," *Studies in New Testament and Early Christian Literature: Essays in Honor of A. P. Wikgren*, ed. D. E. Aune (Leiden: Brill, 1972), pp. 92–103.

N. Perrin, "Wisdom and Apocalyptic in the Message of Jesus," *Society of Biblical Literature 1972 Proceedings*, Vol. 2 (SBL, 1972), pp. 543–572.

L. Goldmann, "Structure: Human Reality and Methodological Concept," *The Languages of Criticism and the Sciences of Man: The Structuralist Controversy* (Baltimore, Md.: Johns Hopkins Press, 1970), pp. 98–110.

W. Barrett, *Zen Buddhism: Selected Writings of D. T. Suzuki* (Garden City, N.Y.: Doubleday, 1956), p. xiv.

77   P. Reps, *Zen Flesh, Zen Bones* (Garden City, N.Y.: Doubleday, n.d.), p. 124.

Wittgenstein, *Tractatus*, #6, p. 522; and F. Waismann, "Notes on Talks with Wittgenstein," *Philosophical Review*, 74 (1965), pp. 12–13, respectively.

78   D. J. Hawkin, "The Incomprehension of the Disciples in the Marcan Redaction," *Journal of Biblical Literature*, 91 (1972), pp. 491–500.

79   Auden, *Collected Longer Poems*, p. 140.

Frye, *Anatomy of Criticism*, p. 90.

Jeremias, *Parables*, pp. 48, 19, respectively.

81   Käsemann, *Perspectives on Paul*, pp. 75, 156, 72, respectively.

M. Heidegger, "Letter on Humanism," *Philosophy in the Twentieth Century*, eds. W. Barrett & H. Aiken (New York: Random House, 1962), pp. 270–302.

B. J. Boelen, "The Question of Ethics in the Thought of Martin Heidegger," *Heidegger and the Quest for Truth*, ed. M. S. Frings (Chicago: Quadrangle Books, 1968), pp. 76–105.

Heidegger, "Letter on Humanism," p. 299.

Stevens, "The Snow Man," *Collected Poems*, p. 10.

The Portable Nietzsche, ed. W. Kaufmann (New York: Viking Press, 1954), p. 454.

95   Dodd, *Parables*, p. 101.

M. Black, "The Parables as Allegory," *Bulletin of the John Rylands Library*, 42 (1960), pp. 273–287.

Jeremias, *Parables*, pp. 71, 74.

J. J. Vincent, "The Parables of Jesus as Self-Revelation," *Studia Evangelica*, I (Berlin: Akademie-Verlag, 1959), pp. 79–99.

Via, *Parables*, p. 134.

97   Lacan, *Structuralism*, pp. 112, 113, respectively.

103   Jeremias, *Parables*, p. 59.

105   E. D. Hirsch, Jr., *Validity in Interpretation* (New Haven: Yale University Press, 1967), p. 263.

W. G. Thompson, *Matthew's Advice to a Divided Community Mt. 17, 22–18,35* (Analecta Biblica, 44; Rome: Biblical Institute Press, 1970).

109   Dodd, *Parables*, p. 17.

111   Jeremias, *Parables*, p. 182.

112   Dodd, *Parables*, p. 94.

Jeremias, *Parables*, p. 139.

Linnemann, *Parables*, p. 86.

114   Via, *Parables*, p. 154.

117   A. B. Lord, *The Singer of Tales* (New York: Atheneum, 1971 = Harvard Studies in Comparative Literature, 24; Harvard University Press, 1960), pp. 26–29, 103–105, 223–234.

Funk, *Language, Hermeneutic, and Word of God*, p. 163.

118   Lord, *Singer*, pp. 101, 155, respectively.

119   C. Lévi-Strauss, *Structural Anthropology* (Garden City, N.Y.: Doubleday, 1967), p. 226.

Bibliographies

The Basic Bibliography for this book is the works cited in the preceding pages of Notes. The following are specialized bibliographies.

BIBLIOGRAPHY 1: METHOD IN HISTORICAL JESUS RESEARCH.

N. Perrin, *Rediscovering the Teaching of Jesus* (London: SCM,1967), pp. 15–53.
W. O. Walker, "The Quest for the Historical Jesus: A Discussion of Methodology," *Anglican Theological Review,* 51 (1969), pp.38–56.
M. D. Hooker, "Christology and Methodology," *New Testament Studies,* 17 (1970–1971), pp. 480–487.
H. K. McArthur, "The Burden of Proof in Historical Jesus Research," *Expository Times,* 82 (1971), pp. 116–119.
D. G. A. Calvert, "An Examination of the Criteria for Distinguishing the Authentic Words of Jesus," *New Testament Studies,* 18 (1971–1972), pp. 209–219.
N. J. McEleney, "Authenticating Criteria and Mk 7:1–23," *Catholic Biblical Quarterly,* 34 (1972), pp. 431–460.

BIBLIOGRAPHY 2: LITERARY CRITICISM AND PARABLES RESEARCH

G. V. Jones, *The Art and Truth of the Parables* (London: S.P.C.K., 1964).
D. O. Via, Jr., *The Parables* (Philadelphia: Fortress Press, 1967).
E. C. Blackman, "New Methods of Parable Interpretation," *Canadian Journal of Theology,* 15 (1969), pp. 3–13.
J. D. Kingsbury, "Ernst Fuch's Interpretation of the Parables," *Lutheran Quarterly,* 22 (1970), pp. 380–395.
———, "Major Trends in Parable Interpretation," *Concordia Theological Monthly,* 42 (1971), pp. 579–596.
———, "The Parables of Jesus in Current Research," *Dialog,* 11 (1972), pp. 101–107.
N. Perrin, "The Parables of Jesus as Parables, as Metaphors, and as Aesthetic Objects: A Review Article," *Journal of Religion,* 47 (1967), pp. 340–347.

————, "The Modern Interpretation of the Parables of Jesus and the Problem of Hermeneutics," *Interpretation*, 25 (1971), pp. 131–148.

————, "Historical Criticism, Literary Criticism, and Hermeneutics: The Interpretation of the Parables of Jesus and the Gospel of Mark Today," *Journal of Religion*, 52 (1972), pp. 361–375.

W. J. Harrington, "The Parables in Recent Study (1960–1971)," *Biblical Theology Bulletin*, 2 (1972), pp. 219–241.

BIBLIOGRAPHY 3: THE ORIGINS OF THE "SON OF MAN" CONCEPT

A. J. B. Higgins, "Son of Man 'Forschung' since *The Teaching of Jesus*," *New Testament Essays: Studies in Memory of T. W. Manson* (Manchester: Manchester University, 1959), pp. 119–135.

M. Black, "The Son of Man Problem in Recent Research and Debate," *Bulletin of the John Rylands Library*, 45 (1962), pp. 305–318.

I. H. Marshall, "The Synoptic Son of Man Sayings in Recent Discussion," *New Testament Studies*, 12 (1965–1966), pp. 327–351.

R. Marlow, "The 'Son of Man' in Recent Journal Literature," *Catholic Biblical Quarterly*, 28 (1966), pp. 20–30.

N. Perrin, *Rediscovering the Teaching of Jesus* (London: SCM, 1967), pp. 164–199 & the annotated bibliography on pp. 259–262.

————, "The Son of Man in the Synoptic Tradition," *Biblical Research*, 13 (1968), pp. 3–25.

I. H. Marshall, "The Son of Man in Contemporary Debate," *Evangelical Quarterly*, 42 (1970), pp. 67–87.

W. O. Walker, Jr., "The Origin of the Son of Man Concept as Applied to Jesus," *Journal of Biblical Literature*, 91 (1972), pp. 482–490.

BIBLIOGRAPHY 4: THE GOSPEL OF THOMAS

O. Cullmann, "The Gospel of Thomas and the Problem of the Age of the Tradition Contained Therein—A Survey," *Interpretation*, 16 (1962), pp. 418–438.

H. Montefiore & H. E. W. Turner, *Thomas and the Evangelists* (Studies in Biblical Theology, 35; Naperville, Ill.: Allenson, 1962).

D. M. Scholer, *Nag Hammadi Bibliography 1948–1969* (Nag Hammadi Studies, 1; Leiden: Brill, 1971), pp. 136–165.

N. Perrin, *Rediscovering the Teaching of Jesus* (London: SCM, 1967). See the bibliography on 253–254.

BIBLIOGRAPHY 5: SELECT BIBLIOGRAPHY FOR THE ENTIRE BOOK

This is a highly select choice of the works which were most helpful in working out the book's discussion.

1. Readings in Philosophy

The philosophical bases of the book are taken from Martin Heidegger. The following is suggested as a step-by-step *approach* to his thought.

S. R. Hopper, "The Poetry of Meaning," *Literature and Religion*, ed. G. B. Gunn (New York: Harper & Row, 1971), pp. 221–235.

N. A. Scott, Jr., *The Wild Prayer of Longing* (New Haven: Yale University Press, 1971), pp. 43–75.

J. M. Robinson, "The German Discussion of the Later Heidegger," *The Later Heidegger and Theology* (New Frontiers in Theology, 1; New York: Harper & Row, 1963), pp. 3–76.

W. B. Macomber, *The Anatomy of Disillusion* (Evanston, Ill.; Northwestern University Press, 1967).

M. Heidegger, "Remembrance of the Poet," and "Hölderlin and the Essence of Poetry," *Existence and Being*, ed. W. Brock (Chicago: Regnery, 1949), pp. 233–269, 270–291.

————, *On the Way to Language* (New York: Harper & Row, 1971).

————, *Poetry, Language, Thought*, ed. A. Hofstadter (New York: Harper & Row, 1971).

————, *On Time and Being* (New York: Harper & Row, 1972).

2. Readings in Literary Criticism

W. A. Shibles, *Metaphor: An Annotated Bibliography and History* (Whitewater, Wis.: Language Press, 1971).

C. Brooks, "Metaphor and the Function of Criticism," *Spiritual Problems in Contemporary Literature* (Gloucester, Mass.: Smith, 1969), pp. 127–137.

M. Krieger, *The New Apologists for Poetry* (Bloomington, Ind.: Indiana University Press, 1963).

J. Hillis Miller, *The Disappearance of God* (New York: Schocken, 1965), pp. 1–10; and also *Poets of Reality* (Cambridge, Mass.: Belknap/Harvard University Press, 1965), pp. 1–12.

P. Wheelwright, *The Burning Fountain* and *Metaphor and Reality* (Bloomington, Ind.: Indiana University Press, 1968 and 1962 respectively).

Metaphor and Symbol, eds. L. C. Knights & B. Cottle (London: Butterworths, 1960).

R. E. Palmer, *Hermeneutics* (Evanston, Ill.: Northwestern University Press, 1969). See, most especially, "A Hermeneutical Manifesto to American Literary Interpretation," on pp. 219–253.

3. Readings in Biblical Exegesis

J. Jeremias, *The Parables of Jesus* (rev. ed.; New York: Scribner, 1963).

D. O. Via, Jr., *The Parables* (Philadelphia: Fortress Press, 1967).

R. W. Funk, *Language, Hermeneutic, and Word of God* (New York: Harper & Row, 1966), pp. 133–162.

J. M. Robinson, "Jesus' Parables as God Happening," *Jesus and the Historian*, ed. F. T. Trotter (Philadelphia: Westminster Press, 1968), pp. 134–150.

Index of Authors

Index of Parables

Index of Citations